"With characteristic flair and refreshing directness, Keisha Gallegos encourages you to stop agonizing over your life's purpose and start finding your mojo. Fun, easy to read and very actionable, this book will help you find your voice and use it to make a difference."
-Pamela Slim, author, Body of Work and Escape From Cubicle Nation

"Keisha Gallegos is a fun new voice in the personal quest for living a passionate life! Thank goodness she discovered her own MOJO ~ lighting human souls on fire! With Keisha's expert intuitive advice, recognizing your destiny is closer then you think."
- **Marie Manuchehri RN**, author of Intuitive Self-Healing

"When a book asks a question like, 'How am I unique and fabulous?', you just know it's going to be a great book. Keisha Gallegos has written a great book, with great questions (and funny stories and witty asides) which will help you uncover who you really are and how you really need to be in this world. The Little Book Of Big MOJO is an instant classic!"
- **Michele Woodward**, Executive Coach and former White House Staff

"If you are looking to have a more joyful, remarkable life, you need to discover your MOJO. Enter Keisha Gallegos, life coach and mojo whisperer, who is going to help you do just that. The Little Book of Big Mojo will give you the intuitive tools and clarity you need to live your life to its greatest potential. Once you know how to access your personal Magical Original Joyful Offering to the world, that marvelous life you dream of (and assume is so-out-of-reach) will be yours."
- **Theresa Reed**, The Tarot Lady

"Author, Keisha Gallegos, brilliantly, humorously, and magically gifts her readers the experience of re-connecting with their MOJO (Magical Original Joyful Offerings). If you desire to reconnect with your true nature, life purpose, and re-claim and share your superpowers, this book is your intravenous injection to get started! Chocked full of bite size wisdom, F-bombs, and overflowing realness! And the best part is the feeling that Keisha is right there, with you all along the way, offering her real, high energy, kick in the pants, loving coaching approach."
- **Denise Hughes**, Certified Money Coach and Dean of the Money School

"Keisha Gallegos has put the "M" back in Mojo. Magical is indeed only part of the brilliance and wisdom of this book. In order to track our "mojo killers" as Ms. Gallegos calls them, she re-frames for us her own unique and inspiring definition of mojo - our "magical, original, joyful, offering to the world." Once we are clear on what's killing our mojo, she takes us step by step through the "antidotes" to bring the spark back into our life and our life's work. Her style and wit is original, sassy, irreverent, and oh so very engaging. An eminently practical and profound "little - big" book."
- **Mary Welty-Dapkus**, Professional Intuitive, Certified Life

"Keisha is a top-tier MOJO magician and Encourager-in-Chief. Follow her wise, witty advice to get your own MOJO back in high gear!"
- **Betsy Rapoport, Editor**, Writer and Master Life Coach

you're got mojo!
yo,
Keisha
Gallegos

The Little Book of Big Mojo

The Secret Decoder Ring to Unleash Your Superpowers

Keisha Gallegos

Certified Master Life Coach

Contents

Introduction

"It is important to remember that we all have magic inside us."
~ JK Rowling

I may be burned as a heretic for saying this, but I'm a little peeved with the human potential movement—and I'm a life coach. While it is well-meaning and earnestly trying to elevate human consciousness, it has inadvertently created an atmosphere of desperation—so many people seem to be beating themselves senseless with the words *what's my life purpose?* Fortunately, most of us aren't consumed with fears of finding a safe place to sleep at night or scavenging enough food to feed our families, so our minds can focus on something beyond survival. We are free to perseverate on the question *why am I here?*

This is the first-world conundrum that wakes us up at night, because we are terrified that we will die without fulfilling our mission. It seems everyone is having an existential crisis, berating ourselves actually, because we are seeking a mystical experience that will tell us in no uncertain terms—with horns blaring, lights flashing, and a voice from the heavens announcing—*This is your calling.* We want a burning bush, a bolt of lightning,

1

a sign so clear that any dumbass could recognize it. I know, I've pleaded with every higher power I could think of to reveal my reason for being put on this earth, and I understand the pain created by not knowing what IT is.

After finally figuring out exactly what my mission was at forty frickin' years old, I was struck by how obvious the clues were when I looked back at my life's path. My goal is to help you figure it out a lot sooner than I did with a method that has worked for hundreds of my clients since I became a life coach in 2009. There is indeed a breadcrumb trail that leads to your personal gift to the world. I call that special sauce your MOJO—your **M**agical, **O**riginal, **J**oyful **O**ffering to the world.

The process of finding your MOJO is one of subtraction rather than addition. We think that if we just learn one more thing, take one more class, or listen to one more speaker we will finally know enough to figure it out. This is bullshit. Here's the deal: your MOJO lives inside of you right now. It's ready to roar, but we've first got to pull off the layers of crap that are strangling it in order to set it free.

I often describe the coaching process as this: picture that you are wearing approximately fifty-three pullover sweaters, one on top of the other. Imagine that you would look like a rotund four-year old in a snowsuit, unable to put your arms down because of your own considerable girth. You are wearing all of these sweaters because you're supposed to, and you're not really sure why, but everyone seems to think it's normal and oh, by the way—it's August. You're sweating, and constrained and miserable and you have no idea why because you've always worn these sweaters and it never occurred to you that you could take them off.

Coaching is the process of removing a few sweaters at a time and noticing the sense of freedom that ensues. We may look at each sweater and wonder who made it for us, or why we wore it for so long, but in the end—that bad boy needs to go. Every painful thought and belief is examined and removed, until you stand tall and proud in your birthday suit as your truest version of yourself. Unencumbered by layers of BS, we can easily feel our MOJO from the tips of our toes to the top of our head. We exude a luminous aura of warmth, confidence, and authenticity.

Have you ever seen the movie *School of Rock*? The story follows struggling rock singer and guitarist Dewey Finn (played convincingly by Jack Black), who is kicked out of his band and subsequently poses as a substitute teacher at a distinguished prep school. Upon realizing that his fourth-grade students possess incredible musical talent, Dewey forms a band to compete in a Battle of the Bands and pay his roommate back the rent money he owes.

I LOVE this movie! You know why? There is MOJO in every frame. Every kid in every scene looks like they are having the time of their life while their "teacher" reflects their own brilliance back to them. Dewey

meets each kid exactly where they are and finds a way
to encourage them to unleash their inner rock star. By
the end of the film, each student has become a more
courageous version of themselves.

Jack Black could not be more fun to watch in this
role—he is hysterical, over the top, and all heart. He's
not the best singer, the best songwriter, the best guitar
player, the most handsome, or even a decent dancer—
but none of that matters. He is mesmerizing because he
is all in, totally committed, and working in his magic
MOJO lane.

The class bossy girl gets the position of "Band
Manager"—how perfect! A flamboyant boy with a flair
for style becomes the band costume designer. Another
with amazing technical skills programs the light show.
Everyone had a place to shine, and each was important.
That's how I see the world: everyone has an important
role to play and is capable of being great in his or her
own unique way.

While reading this book, think of me as Jack Black's
character Dewey Finn—a highly sensitive detector of
your gifts and talents, your encourager-in-chief, and a
wild magnifier of your MOJO. I want to take you on a
fantastic MOJO recovery voyage, where we will reclaim
all of the very best gifts you hold inside of you.

Each of the fifteen MOJO killers listed in this book
are tantamount to wearing several ill-fitting, scratchy
sweaters. Once you know what's destroying your
MOJO, you can take the antidote and rip those sweaters

off! Your MOJO is not OUT THERE, waiting for you to find it. Your MOJO is right under your nose, inside you, where it's been overlooked and undervalued.

*Some important notes about how to use this book...I beg of you, PLEASE DO THE EXERCISES!!! Without your introspection and subsequent action, nothing in your life will change. Your participation in this process is required for growth—you can do it!!! I'm here to cheer you on.

Clients' first names and identifying information were changed to protect their privacy. Friends' names were kept in tact to make them famous!

My proofreader and co-editor, Lynn Blaney Hess, will plot my untimely death if I do not mention that I will be using they/their rather than the proper pronouns per my conversational tone. This was reluctantly agreed to by her as long as I agreed to explain that this was purposeful and not just bad grammar! Also, I would like to acknowledge that my book coach and co-editor Laura Wooten's Midwestern sensibilities were flustered at my using the word "fuck" in print. I would like to take full responsibility for this and absolve her of any blame or judgment incurred by my actions.

Now that we've cleared all that up—c'mon, we've got important shit to do!

Chapter 1:
What is MOJO?

"Don't ask what the world needs. Ask what makes you come alive and go do it. Because what the world needs is people who have come alive."
~ Howard Thurman

MOJO is a state of mind. It's the way you do the things you do. It's an art, not a science. It's the sparkle in your eye and the spring in your step.

The traditional definition of MOJO is *"an amulet, charm or magic spell"* or an *"uncanny personal power or influence."* Today MOJO is used interchangeably with confidence, charisma, cool, swag, or passion. Lots of people think of Austin Powers when they think about MOJO (yeah baby, yeah!).

My definition of MOJO is an acronym:

Magical
Original
Joyful
Offering to the world.

While lots of people think about MOJO as a quality of being that they want to recapture—as in "I need to get my MOJO back"—my definition of MOJO is that it's your unique secret sauce, so it can never really be lost. It is your own personal power that you can replicate over and over again. Of course, you have to know exactly what your special brand of MOJO is before you can replicate it. And that's what you will know by the time you finish this book!

Show Me the MOJO— What MOJO Looks Like

Do you know when your MOJO is flowing? If not, it is helpful to have an example of what MOJO looks and feels like.

MOJO is the way that Elvis swiveled his hips, the way Cher tosses her hair while licking her lips. MOJO is Marilyn Monroe's mixture of vulnerability and sex appeal. It's Madonna's unapologetic brazenness and Michael Jackson's moonwalk. It's Beyoncé's syncopated songs of female empowerment, Ellen DeGeneres' charm and wit, and Jon Stewart's ability to highlight the ironic and the moronic.

MOJO is Mick Jagger's strut, Tina Turner's strength, Lady Gaga's eccentric performance art. It's the way Steve Jobs delivered a keynote for a new Apple product, and Sir Richard Branson's excitement and pride in all things Virgin. It's Johnny Depp's swagger in any role he plays (especially the ones where he wears a costume and makeup!).

MOJO means you are **all in**. You are committed. You are impervious to fear about how others will see or judge you. Think Will Ferrell or Jim Carrey—they don't care how stupid, how naked, how ridiculous they come off or if you get the joke. They will go to any lengths to make a character completely ludicrous so they can get the biggest laugh.

MOJO is not only for the young. Helen Mirren, sexy in her sixties—more MOJO. Betty White, still hilarious in her nineties? Red hot MOJO—bucking the myth of becoming irrelevant as she ages. Diane Keaton has incorporated her self-consciousness and self-deprecation into her MOJO—we can't help but fall in love with her. Meryl Streep is having more fun than ever in her performances; she proudly wears her age and experience, which makes for seriously powerful MOJO.

MOJO is not just for actors and rock stars. I recently witnessed a busboy at a great restaurant with crazy good MOJO. This guy was like a tornado—he whipped through the restaurant like a whirling dervish. He cleaned those tables with such style, originality, and commitment! You would have thought the President was coming with the attention to detail and elbow grease he put into preparing the tables for his customers. He attended to our water glasses frequently and carefully in very broken English, with loving care and pride in his work. I was highly impressed by this guy's work ethic and intense focus; he should give classes on how to do a great job. It inspires me to witness people in all professions *do their thang* with flair and flourish. It's the way you do the things you do!

Politicians need to work their MOJO to get elected. Kennedy displayed his good looks and charisma and promised a new America to win over voters. Carter used his affable and honest character to reassure the country after the scandal of Watergate and Nixon's resignation had created much cynicism in many Americans. Reagan showcased his comforting presence and skills as "the great communicator."

"Slick Willy" Clinton had an amazing ability to make everyone he met feel important and he dazzled the electorate with his combination of charm and intelligence. The pendulum swung the opposite way with George W. Bush—his appeal was his straight-shooter demeanor mixed with being the guy who people would most like to have a beer with.

Obama brought hope for change to the country after wars in the Middle East, a massive economic collapse, and with the pain of 9/11 still fresh. His unflappable optimism and ability to articulate it created a swell of voter involvement not seen in several generations.

Now, you would have to agree that these politicians are all very different and stand for many different (even opposite) things, and you may strongly agree with some of their ideas more than others. But, regardless of what causes they have championed, what they do have in common is that they connected to their MOJO in a big way to try to accomplish their agendas.

What MOJO Is Not

MOJO does not copy. It does not take polls about what's popular. It does not criticize others. MOJO isn't about perfection; it's about originality and flair. It's passion, confidence, swag, and dedication all rolled into one. It's the divine spark of creativity in all of us, and the courage to follow it through.

MOJO isn't cultivated; it's unleashed.

MOJO isn't your new haircut or new outfit; it's how you feel about wearing it.

It's the feeling of badass when you know you are rockin'. It's your sparkle, your light, your complete disregard for fitting in based on superficial measurements of failure or success.

Why Does MOJO Matter?

You might be saying to yourself, *well, so what? I have no desire to be a movie star or a megalomaniac.*

It matters because finding your MOJO means finding your own way to more freedom and joy.

Your Original Medicine

The more you engage your magical, original, joyful offering to the world, the more your MOJO multiplies. Indigenous cultures call this our "original medicine." In this context, medicine means power. Throughout this book, we will be going about the task of searching for your original medicine—finding the gift that is yours and uniquely yours that you were meant to bring to this world.

The moment you recognize what constitutes your own MOJO, you can begin using it in everything you do. No more conforming, no more making yourself small, no more doubting your gifts. You may doubt that your MOJO is original. You may say, "But Yolanda is a wayyyy better writer than I am," or "I'll never be able to give a presentation as well as Kirk," or "No one can match Skeeter's brilliance as a taxidermist!" Of course, there are others who have similar gifts—but not one of those people embody those gifts in the same exact and beautiful way that you do.

You may not believe this, but an integral part of your MOJO is probably something that you've tried to change about yourself to make it easier to fit in. One thing is universal about our MOJO: it is built on a foundation of authenticity. *Always.*

My Affinity for MOJO

I have always felt a bit peculiar because I feel things so deeply. I wear my heart on my sleeve and cannot hide my emotions to save my life. I'm quite vivacious, and very animated when I speak. I make lots of silly faces and I gesticulate wildly to get my point across. I have been told that I should have my own set of emoticons based on the wide variety of facial expressions I use.

I have understood this to be part of my passionate personality, and the way I express myself is equally passionate. But what I couldn't understand was why I fought back tears the moment Disney On Ice would begin or at the beautiful opening scene of The Lion King. I've felt overcome with emotion while watching a concert where one of my favorite performers is singing his heart out, or watching an Olympic gymnast nail her routine after a lifetime of preparation.

I've become verklempt while watching a dedicated teacher give a lesson, or witnessing a veterinarian gently caring for a scared dog. I have been known to tear up watching *Shark Tank* when an inventor is excitedly pitching his or her product in hopes of attracting investors.

What do all of these situations have in common that make me feel so much? These people are wholeheartedly working their MOJO, which (according to me) is their Magical Original Joyful Offering to the world. And evidently, watching MOJO in action makes me cry.

I used to be embarrassed at my "ridiculous" emotional response to watching someone unabashedly work a skill with exuberance and heart. I was actually ashamed at my depth of feeling. Now I realize that this was a clue that highlights my own MOJO. It fires me up inside to watch people excel in a way that feeds their soul and makes them so shiny I can't look away.

Along the way, I discovered that I can coax mojo out of the damnedest places. Places where most of us forget to look, or have lost the map to entirely. Other people may dismiss someone who lacks confidence or bravado as plain or uninteresting. Not me. Like a chocoholic can find a candy shop, I can find anyone's MOJO; in fact I have yet to find a person whose own unique MOJO potion I cannot identify. The funniest part is that it's usually been hiding in plain sight, just waiting to be unveiled.

Why Should I Listen to You, Lady?

How do I know? Because I found my own MOJO, which is **helping you find your MOJO**.

I'm Keisha Gallegos—the MOJO Whisperer.

I love nothing more than to help people get their MOJO back. In fact, it's the request I get from most of my clients. I've realized from coaching hundreds of people that finding and magnifying MOJO is actually what I do best. It's my gift.

I Lost My MOJO

Back in 2008 I was a sorry sight.

Three of my most important relationships were in the crapper...my sister and I weren't speaking, things with my best friend were going downhill fast, and my husband and I were ready to kill each other. My sons were thirteen and sixteen then, well into the "I'm embarrassed I even have parents" stage.

I was in my seventh year of working at a low-paying job that was challenging only to my nerves rather than my skill set, because I'd spent the past sixteen years raising my family, not pursuing my dream career. I'd willingly sacrificed my own personal goals to support my husband's career, run our household, and be a mother.

I was banging my head against the wall every day trying to figure out what I was doing wrong. Why couldn't I figure out what I wanted to be when I grew up?

I was depressed, confused, and pissed off.

Then one day I did something "selfish."

I went to Oprah Winfrey's all-day *O You!* seminar that featured experts in various fields who write for her magazine. I specifically went to see Dr. Martha Beck. Every month I would read her intoxicating blend of Harvard science mixed with spirituality and a large dose of humor. Her books *Finding Your Own North Star* and *Steering By Starlight* are what I now call the "life coaching bible"—old and new testament. She gave me a template for how to handle life's challenges and crossroads with grace and self-compassion.

Halfway through her speech, she spoke about her love of training life coaches, and a flash of possibility jolted through me. I had a life-changing moment right then—everything around me became fuzzy, I could no longer hear her talking, and every fiber of my being shouted, "This is what I am meant to do!" It was *a struck by lightning, turn your world upside down* epiphany. I sat stunned in the audience as she finished her speech, dumbstruck. This was the revelation I had been waiting for.

What if I could be a life coach?

I was *usually* someone who had my shit together. I've always been the problem solver, compassionate ear, and encouraging cheerleader for my family and friends. I had always loved nothing more than helping people close to me make brave steps, define boundaries, and believe in themselves. Now if I could only do those things for myself.

I took what felt like a huge personal risk and enrolled in Martha's program—even though I was full of terror and self-doubt. *Would anyone really hire me to coach them?* Before I went through my coach training, I really thought that only famous people had life coaches. I had no idea I was joining a burgeoning industry just about to bust wide open.

The economy was in shambles and financial

institutions were collapsing daily. There was change on the horizon as President Obama had just been elected and the fear in the air was palpable. People who'd had steady jobs for their entire lives were being laid off in droves, and businesses we thought would survive forever were closing their doors. It felt like a game of musical chairs where everyone was scrambling for security before the music stopped.

What a great time to start a new business, right?!?!?!?!?!

I Led a Double Life

Up until then, I had two jobs—the job I told everyone about and the one I hid. Everyone around me knew I worked as a substitute teacher at my children's school. But most people had no idea that I also worked as an intuitive (yes, psychic) for private clients. I was very uncomfortable telling others about my intuitive skills, lest I be judged or ridiculed. I wanted my kids to have a normal childhood, without having to answer for what their turban-wearing, crystal ball-toting mom did for a living. (Just kidding about the turban; in fact, when my clients would meet me at my front door for a reading, they were always relieved to see how "normal" I looked.) While I loved giving people readings, I hated how some clients would give up all their power because they just wanted me to tell them what to do. I was really uncomfortable with that because what I really loved doing was helping my clients feel empowered to forge their own destiny, not just endure their fate. Strictly giving intuitive readings just never felt complete to me, so I cut back my practice and yearned for something more—if only I knew what that was.

When I began seeing life-coaching clients in 2009, I knew I had found my calling. Not only was I able to capitalize on the left-brain skills I had spent so many years practicing as a teacher and a mom (lesson planning, public speaking, and positive reinforcement!), I was quietly using my intuitive skills with the awesome tools I had learned in my training to lead people out of their own way and on to more freedom and joy. Helping people to reach their highest potential by busting past obstacles in a fun but soulful way was beyond thrilling for me. I felt light and excited before my clients arrived, lost track of time during my sessions, and afterward felt a profound sense of meaning and purpose. I had found my MOJO!

I'm Out and I'm Proud

Today I am happier and more fulfilled than I ever thought possible. My husband Alex and I just celebrated our twenty-fourth anniversary, and he has been inspired by my success to throw off his corporate shackles and start his own business. My boys are now young men who've proudly watched me build a thriving coaching practice from the ground up. I came out of the intuitive closet to my life-coaching clients several years ago, and I was pleasantly surprised (actually, shocked) that they a) didn't care, b) found it interesting and were curious, or c) thought it was freakin' awesome—two skills for the price of one! It felt so good to stop hiding and finally fully embrace my intuitive self. Putting my guard down and allowing people to really know me has enhanced my life in more ways than I could have ever imagined.

Not only have my core relationships with my husband and family become even better since I found my MOJO through coaching, but I also have the most amazing group of new people in my life now—people who inspire me daily, make me laugh, and are living examples that anything is possible. Some of my best friends are other coaches, people who add to my life in ways I never could have predicted.

The biggest difference in my circle of friends is that everyone around me is interested in learning and growing, which I've discovered are fundamental values to me. Birds of a feather definitely flock together, and since I spend so much of my time on coaching-related endeavors, my people are a posse of positive, giving, and pretty effing magical peeps! And NONE of this would have happened if I hadn't made that huge leap in the darkness in 2008.

The Universe has conspired to assist me since I made up my mind and got out of my own way.

How I Became the MOJO Whisperer...

A few years into my practice, I noticed that people who reached out to me for a consultation often said the same thing: "I feel like I've lost my MOJO." And after clients had worked with me for a bit, I would hear "I'm finding my MOJO!"

I realized that I was, in fact, a MOJO whisperer. I could lure MOJO out of hiding for people who didn't know they ever had any MOJO, or who couldn't spot their own MOJO if their life depended on it. I discovered that I could spot just a wisp of MOJO and go in and excavate for more.

I believe everyone has MOJO, whether it's been hidden under pain, suffering, bills, and obligation—or if it was forgotten long ago in your youth. Everybody in the whole world has their own special brand of MOJO—and I'm going to show you how to find yours.

Who Is Your MOJO Idol?

Who's your MOJO idol? Is that a tough one to answer? Try asking yourself who you pretended to be as a kid. Who did you mimic in the mirror when you were home alone in your room?

I remember pretending I was Jamie from *The Bionic Woman*, Samantha from *Bewitched*, Jeannie from *I Dream of Jeannie*, and Jaclyn Smith's character Kelly from *Charlie's Angels* (the TV show, not the movie. Yes, the original one. From the '70s. I know…) And while we're going wayyyyyy back, I may as well tell you that I used to put on masterful performances as Cher while wearing a heavily safety-pinned polyester nightgown of my mother's while holding a plastic jump rope in lieu of a microphone. (Not quite the Bob Mackie professional designs the real Cher wore on her TV show—but hey, I was six years old.) I begged my mother to let me wear her clear roller ball lip-gloss that smelled like strawberries to complete the look because seriously, what's a Cher impersonator without lip gloss?

What did these '60s and '70s icons all have in common? They were badass mamajamas. Strong, beautiful women who had SUPERPOWERS! Jamie Summers was bionic, Samantha Stevens was a witch, Jeannie was—well, a genie. Jaclyn Smith was a powerful crime fighter who hung out with her other hot friends in cool clothes.

Cher was different-looking from any other woman on television. She was ethnic, far from the Waltons and the Bradys. Cher didn't sing like anyone else, and she wore amazing costumes with flair and had more confidence than any woman I had ever seen. Cher didn't have the best voice, nor was she the best dancer or the most beautiful. In fact she had a little mustachioed dude (whom she didn't seem to like very much) as her husband. What she did have was ownership of the stage. I wanted some of that power as a kid.

You—As a Superhero

Maybe for you it was an action hero like Luke Skywalker or Indiana Jones. Or a superhero like Batman or Superman or Wonder Woman. Or was it your favorite professional athlete, Olympian, or martial artist?

Did you know that by using powerful body language you can trick your brain into feeling confident? Put your hands on your hips, and place your feet hip distance apart (à la Superman) for two minutes and you'll invoke your inner superhero when you're feeling crappy, and save the day!

Need some sassy energy? Channel Beyoncé (one of my mojo idols!). Need some courage? Channel your favorite action hero. Not sure how to move forward with something difficult? Channel your favorite mentor, teacher, or boss!

Halloween is a day to role play. When you were a child, who did you dress up as? If you go to Halloween parties now, do you have a favorite costume to wear or character you love to play? Your subconscious is speaking to you when you gravitate toward a certain genre; allow it to guide you to your MOJO model!

Another method—and this will probably sound strange to you—is to ask yourself who you were jealous of as a kid. And, who do you envy now? Come on, you can admit it. The green-eyed monster comes out to play with everyone at some point. But here's a new way of looking at it: jealousy is a fantastic vehicle for figuring out your MOJO heroes. The emotions of envy and jealousy show you what you value and what you want more of…and if you use them correctly, these feelings can show you how to get it.

MOJO in Motion...

Answer these questions…
Who do you respect and want to emulate?

_____

Why do you want to be more like them?

_____

What are their MOJO-full qualities?

_____

What do they have that you wish that you possessed?

_____

Who did you think you would be when you grew up?

_____

Now that you have some examples of MOJO idols for yourself, notice the characteristics that you most value about them. Where do you see those same traits in yourself? Even if you don't embody them all the time, I'll bet there have been times where you've amazed yourself with your own MOJO. Once you have identified the qualities you value in others, you can amp them up in yourself.

For example, I really love watching Jimmy Fallon on *The Tonight Show*.

What are the qualities I like? His playfulness, his inability to take himself too seriously, his spot-on impressions, and his courage to go balls-out every night on national television with new material. Oh, and he's FUNNY!

Where do I have some of the qualities I value in Jimmy Fallon? Well, I am a tremendously gifted goofball. I definitely don't take myself too seriously, and I have become more courageous in putting my ideas (like this book!) out into the world; this makes me vulnerable to possible criticism, but also has the potential to help people, and my willingness may embolden others to do the same. I'm also a wicked mimic—and my dogs think I'm funny.

How can I amp these qualities up in myself? Very simply, I can stay off the freaky hamster wheel in my mind (which writer Anne Lamott likens to "a bad neighborhood that I try not to go into alone.") Yes, I'm asking you to stop overthinking everything. We humans can talk ourselves out of anything if we give ourselves enough time. We are in a no-MOJO zone when we spend too much time calculating and not enough time acting. At some point, we've got to put our analysis into action—we must create opportunities to allow our awesome attributes to take flight.

To be clear, I am not trying to copy Jimmy Fallon. I am amplifying in myself the aspects of him that I admire, because we always have a little of what we value in others in ourselves. We wouldn't recognize it otherwise.

So, I look for occasions to pull out my playfulness. I check myself when I find that I am taking myself too seriously. (How do I know when I'm doing that? When my brow is wrinkled, I'm mentally cataloging all the ways something could go wrong, or basically any time I am in a place of fear rather than love.) I hang out with people who laugh, who are funny, and who think I'm funny! Get the picture? Now you try...

My MOJO idol is…..

_____

What qualities do I like about my MOJO idol?

_____

Where do I have some of the qualities that I admire in my MOJO idol?

_____

How can I amp up some of these qualities in myself?

_____

Does my MOJO idol's profession give me any clues about what line of work I'd like to pursue?

_____

Chapter 2:
M is for Magical

"By choosing to be our most authentic and loving self,
we leave a trail of magic wherever we go."
~ *Emmanuel Dagher*

A good magician can make the most difficult trick look effortless. With a smile, a wave of the hand, and an abracadabra, he can pull a rabbit out of a hat. The magician doesn't sweat, screw up his face in concentration, or complain to his audience about how hard it is to pull off a challenging illusion. He carries out his sleight of hand elegantly, as if it took no exertion whatsoever.

I believe every one of us has magical properties, and that those qualities are the ingredients in your own personal MOJO recipe. Rather than searching for and dwelling on the parts of yourself that require improving, how about noticing the abilities that come easily to you, as if by magic.

You've Got Magic in You

One definition of magical is to "mysteriously enchant." Another is "the art of invoking supernatural powers to influence people or events." When we connect to the most magical part of ourselves, we can create desired results with ease and grace. We simply *allow* the magic to come through us—we allow ourselves to be used in the best possible way.

Where do you have the ability to influence people or events? What do you think your strongest asset is? What do other people who you trust tell you about you? What feedback have you received? Is it your ability to stay calm when everyone else is freaking out? Your fantastic smile or the way you make people feel at ease? Maybe it's your sense of humor, or your genuine caring for other people. Start with where you feel the most comfortable, because you might find some MOJO hiding there.

How Are You Magical?

Remember the scene in *Cinderella* where the mice create a ball gown for "Cinderelly" by scavenging odds and ends throughout the house? Those magical mice made a gorgeous dress from almost nothing. You know how to do that in some aspect of your life.

Can you make an amazing meal with the last 5 ingredients in the refrigerator? Can you "MacGyver" a solution to a problem with a paperclip, a book of matches, and a piece of gum? Can you get a party started with some music, a bottle of wine, and your mere presence?

Maybe you can broker peace between warring factions of your family because you are a natural mediator, or soothe a colicky baby because you know how to softly hum a relaxing tune and jounce the little bugger just right. Are you the person your friends and family call to negotiate a good deal on a car or electronics? Perhaps you are the family travel agent or resident researcher. Basically, what does everyone ask you to do because you are really good at it? That's a clue to your magic MOJO.

The Way You Do the Things You Do

Your MOJO is the way you do the things you do. It's not just about your skills and talents. It's about the attitude and quality of the energy you bring to any task. It's about how you captivate an audience, the charismatic way you influence people, or your knack for bringing a quiet and calming wisdom to a tense situation. Maybe you can fix *anything*, garden like a mo-fo, write killer computer code, or whip an accounting ledger into shape like no one else. All MOJO is valuable MOJO!

I have a client named Will who I call my "mogul" because I am so impressed with how many business ventures he always has going at the same time. When I asked him what he thought his superpower was, he told me it was his ability to "get shit done." And he *does*. That guy does more with his allotted twenty-four hours in a day than most people do in a week. He's efficient, responsive, and thorough. He moves with a purpose. Will doesn't mess around—he gets right on tasks and spends no time dilly-dallying. To me he is the epitome of the Ben Franklin quote "If you want something done, ask a busy person." It might not seem very glamorous, but getting shit done quickly and correctly is crazy good MOJO!

Who Would You Have Been in the 1500s?

Another entertaining way to look at this is to ask, "What would my Renaissance-era job be?" Before the world of work became as complicated as it is today, there were very limited career selections available (especially for women). In addition to a few others I'll mention in a minute, there were farmers, hunters, stonemasons, soldiers, cooks, bakers, butchers, blacksmiths, priests and nuns, scholars, teachers, bankers, magistrates, and law enforcers…and not too many other choices! So, imagine yourself back then, and pretend you had to pick one of these very limited choices. What would you have been? The profession you choose might not be exactly what you want to do now, but it can give you valuable hints about the direction you naturally gravitate toward and lead you to a modern-day offshoot.

Merchants of the past are today's sales professionals. Rulers are executives, managers, and politicians. Inventors are scientists, entrepreneurs, and content creators. Shepherds are people who tend—animal rescuers, dog walkers, organizers, and administrative assistants. Jesters are comedians, marketing geniuses, and snappy copywriters. Cobblers and tailors are clothing designers. Artists are hair stylists, tattoo artists, interior decorators, makeup artists, and jewelry designers. Servants are service professionals and technicians. Healers aren't just doctors, nurses, and paramedics, but also therapists, life coaches, energy workers, massage therapists, shamans, and intuitives. Mothers are caregivers, and so are daycare providers, home health care workers, office managers, personal assistants, and human resource professionals.

The number of career choices available to us now is staggering. Better health, longer life expectancy, more equality for women, better educational opportunities, and less focus on basic survival are wonderful, but have created an atmosphere that fosters the existential crises (aka "What the hell is my life purpose?") we see an epidemic of today. We have "first world" problems now, and finding our MOJO is one of the most common. But I promise you—no matter how distant or out-of-reach your magical MOJO seems, you DO have it in you— and once you uncover it, having all these modern-day choices will serve you very well in deciding how to use it.

MOJO in Motion

What qualities do you possess that feel effortless to you?

_____

What is your strongest asset?

_____

What do other people say about you?

_____

Who are you to others?

_____

What do people ask you to do for them?

_____

What would your Renaissance job be?

_____

Chapter 3:
O is for Original

"The more you like yourself, the less you are like anyone else, which makes you unique."
~ *Walt Disney*

Your MOJO is the most original part of you. It's your essence. It's who you would be no matter where you lived, what culture you belonged to, what school you went to, or what family you were a part of.

Your MOJO could be your way of thinking about things. It could be your energy. It could be a skill that you may completely ignore or brush off because you think it's no big deal or that "everyone can do that if they try."

Easy and Special Are Not Mutually Exclusive

You may think they are because something is easy *for you*. We think that just because a thing is easy for us means it's easy for everyone. Not so—not even close. My sister Dana decorates gorgeous sugar cookies that are little works of art. She has a steady hand to create beautiful designs with, and oodles of patience, not to mention creativity and artistic ability; in other words, she has crazy cool cookie baker MOJO. Sadly, I did not receive that talent when God was handing out the MOJO. I can barely play Pictionary without being lynched by my teammates because my artistic skills are so bad. Cookie artistry is a natural talent and practiced skill for my sister, not so much for me.

However, Dana marvels at my ability to host a dinner party and life coaching workshop for 15–30 women at my house every month *for over five years*. She thinks I'm batshit crazy (in a loving way!) for doing it because she doesn't really dig entertaining all that much. I'm pretty good at it, and I never really thought of it as a skill—more that I'm just wacko enough to not only sign on for such a labor-intensive undertaking, but to enjoy it. Who knew? I've got hospitality MOJO!

Who Are You to Other People?

I always ask my clients to notice what people say about them. It's a huge indicator you may be missing that could give you valuable information about your MOJO. What do they compliment you on? What do they say is something that you do better than anyone else? What are you known for?

What Have You Been Mocked For?

Your originality may even be the part of you that people make fun of. When I was growing up, I was known for being really, really sensitive—about everything. I would cry when I watched the news because I had such deep empathy for people I'd never met. I would say my prayers at night and include the suffering people I had seen on TV.

I was physically sensitive too. My grandmother thought I was faking it when I told her that hot dogs and salami gave me a headache (ever heard of nitrates?). I could feel it in my body when anyone close to me was sad or hurting, and I felt personally responsible for their feelings. I was shattered when my parents were angry or disappointed in me. Family members routinely told me I was too sensitive, too emotional, and too vulnerable. I needed to "toughen up," they said.

Well, look at me now. I make a living out of being sensitive because it's a part of my being and is part of why I'm a really good intuitive and coach. I am very in touch with my feelings and emotions, which helps me teach my clients to be connected to themselves. My vulnerability is one of the things people say they like most about me. I'm willing to tell people how I really feel, and to talk about tough subjects so that my friends and clients get to know me and thus learn to know and accept themselves.

I'm willing to be brave first and let people know who I really am—the gooey center, not the crispy shell on the outside. My desire to help other people led me to become a coach—to help my clients see the best in themselves and to become capable of reaching their goals and making their own dreams come true.

This is *who* I am, it's *what* I am. No matter what kind of upbringing I would have had or what life circumstances may have come my way, I could not have changed that about me. At times I didn't like my sensitive side and it was something I wished I could change. It would have been easier to be tough when I was bullied at school or punished at home, but I just wasn't capable. Now I realize that, for me, being sensitive IS being strong. It is who I am and it is a characteristic that is foundational.

Feeling things strongly can be seen as being courageous, passionate, and wholehearted in the positive sense. On the negative side, I can also be a canary in the coal mine, vulnerable to attack by all things that are too much. I need to be careful about my mental health because my sensitivity makes me prone to clinical depression—which means I limit my exposure to negativity I cannot control. The news, angry people, violence (both real and imagined on TV, movies, or video games), or nasty talk radio are things I avoid like the plague. I must be cognizant of what uplifts and energizes me, and make anything that fits that description part of my daily life.

I choose to love this part of myself, because to change it would be to alter something perfect and beautiful in myself. I understand now that my capacity for empathy is part of my MOJO, and I am proud of it. It's my superpower, biotttchh!

MOJO in Motion...

Name a quality or ability that you are known for and may even have been mocked for:

_____

Is it something that feels intrinsic to your identity?

_____

Is there a skill you have that you dismiss as being easy, but others may have a hard time with?

_____

These things are markers of MOJO—follow them!

Chapter 4:
J is for Joyful

"When you are joyful, when you say yes to life and have fun and project positivity all around you, you become a sun in the center of every constellation, and people want to be near you."
~ *Shannon L. Alder*

Joyfulness is a crucial part of your MOJO. When you are involved in any activity that brings you joy, you are hot on the track of your MOJO. Feeling happy and excited about what you are engaged in is letting you know that you're getting warmer and warmer, like that game of hot and cold you played as a kid. When you're having fun, losing track of time, and engrossed in what you're doing—PAY ATTENTION! There is MOJO afoot!

MOJO Might Be Right Under Your Nose

All my life I could (and still do!) spend hours with my girlfriends, either talking on the phone or physically hanging out. My favorite thing has always been problem solving to help make things better for them. I love encouraging my friends, helping them find solutions to their issues, and empowering them to see that they are capable and deserving of more in their lives.

In the past I have had my fair share of friends who were what I would call "projects." I'm not proud of it, but at times I subconsciously collected people who were overly needy or unable to give back. These particular friends were people I felt I could help—and it made me feel good about myself to be useful. What I really liked about these friendships was how I felt about myself when I was operating at what I felt was my peak state. I felt euphoric about helping people break through obstacles that were holding them back.

What didn't feel euphoric was, when I was having troubles of my own, realizing that these friends were mostly unable or unwilling to help me. Sometimes I would even pair up with someone who I knew couldn't help me and whose help I wouldn't take even if they offered it—because I just liked being their person. We were mismatched, which fed my need to please but left me drained when my time came for support and they weren't capable of really helping me. And although I meant well, making someone my "project" was also really disempowering for them. I wasn't honoring their journey by allowing them to be exactly who they were.

When I began my career in coaching, the helper/cheerleader/encourager part of myself was on cloud nine! Now there's an actual exchange of energy when I'm coaching someone. I give them my full attention, care, insight, and skill as a coach and they pay me for my time. I realized that I had been a frustrated coach all my life, but never knew there was a career for me that encompassed my best natural skills and my original talents. I feel sheer joy when I help someone over a hurdle that's been plaguing their psyche and keeping them stuck. I am able to use my best traits skillfully with people who actually want my help and happily pay me for it. It is so much more fulfilling than helping one of my "projects," and much more loving to everyone involved.

Part of what I love to do now with clients who are searching for their MOJO is to take them to their most joyous moments and find the patterns of what those moments have in common. If you look throughout your life and notice what has brought you the most fulfillment, you will see that there is a pattern. Notice if there is an overall theme to what brings you joy.

MOJO in Motion...

Name five of the most joyful moments
you can remember:
1)
2)
3)
4)
5)

Get quiet and still for a moment and envision yourself
back in each of these moments, and ask yourself:

What are you doing?

_____

Where are you excelling?

_____

When you were in this state of joy, how did you feel like
you were being used in the most positive sense of the
word?

_____

Notice that in many of your most joyful moments,
you are able to be completely yourself. You are FREE!

Chapter 5:
O is for Offering

"I am not trying to change the world. I am just offering my gift that God gave me, and if somebody is moved by it, that's beautiful."
~ Lenny Kravitz

Offering is the final part of your MOJO. When you offer your magical, original, joyful self up, you are giving the world a gift. You've gotta put your MOJO out there. It's no good if you keep it to yourself! The world needs more MOJO.

MOJO in a Perfect World

Imagine, if you will, a world where everyone is rockin' their MOJO. Everyone is using their gifts for the greater good. There is a plethora of authenticity, originality, joy, and magic. The common practice of comparing ourselves to others has gone by the wayside and we all appreciate the beauty and uniqueness that we possess, and honor that in others.

We know that we are enough. We have forgotten how to hustle for our self-worth. We soon realize that it is good for everyone when we embrace our genius and broadcast it out to the Universe—because we need it. We welcome the brilliance that each of us brings and we all benefit when someone else offers up the full expression of who they are.

No one wins when fantastic people hide their light. Every invention, every design, every piece of art, every song, every book, every movie, every theory, every nugget of knowledge came to the collective consciousness because someone was brave enough to put themselves out there. Someone was brazen enough to think their idea mattered.

Historic MOJO

Where would we be if Thomas Edison had stopped trying the 9,999th time he tried to make a working light bulb? Sheer tenacity, passion, and dedication allowed him to carry on day after day, failure after failure. We love stories of perseverance and strength; they inspire us to keep going after our own setbacks and disappointments.

What are you holding back from the world? It doesn't have to be some life-altering invention. Mother Teresa made her entire life about compassion. Fierce compassion. Oprah Winfrey built her career around vulnerability—when she spoke about unspeakable things in her life, it helped others to do the same. Steve

Jobs' MOJO was integrating complex technology with beautiful, intuitive, and simple design—he didn't invent the computer, he made it easier to use. Elvis didn't invent rock and roll music, but he brought it to the masses through incredibly powerful charisma and originality.

Just Be You

You don't have to reinvent the wheel, you just need to make it your special design. Allow your quirks and strangeness to be free and be vocal. With each act of courage on your part, you give someone else permission to be a bit more of who they are. We must shake off critics and plow through disappointment.

Vulnerability researcher Brené Brown titled her book *Daring Greatly* after Theodore Roosevelt's "Man in the Arena" speech:

> *"It is not the critic who counts; not the man who points out how the strong man stumbles, or where the doer of deeds could have done them better. The credit belongs to the man who is actually in the arena, whose face is marred by dust and sweat and blood; who strives valiantly; who errs, who comes short again and again, because there is no effort without error and shortcoming; but who does actually strive to do the deeds; who knows great enthusiasms, the great devotions; who spends himself in a worthy cause; who at the best knows in the end the triumph of high achievement, and who at the worst, if he fails, at least*

*fails while **daring greatly**, so that his place shall never be with those cold and timid souls who neither know victory nor defeat."*

Don't be a cold and timid soul. Go out there and get knocked on your ass. Then go out there and do it again. You'll find that the hardest part of the journey is the first step. It's all downhill after that. Making the decision to be bold and honest is difficult, but making the first step is the most fear-provoking step you will take.

But it's the good kind of fear. It looks like "I've never done this before. I'm out here without a net and I don't know if it's going to be successful. But I'm here and I'm taking the next step!" Yes, you will feel exposed, and yes, you will feel vulnerable. But at least you are feeling something!

Thoreau said that "the mass of men lead lives of quiet desperation." But that is not what we're here for—we are meant to live joyfully and, in doing so, share the best of who we are with the word. In the words of Oliver Wendell Holmes, "Alas for those that never sing, but die with all their music in them!" Alas, indeed. Don't let it happen to you. Sing your song!

Carolyn's MOJO Story

"My massage is 'different.'"
~ *Carolyn Ulitsky, Intuitive muscle therapist,*
Energy worker, Angel magnet

Carolyn came to see me after attending one of my events. She wanted to expand her massage therapy business and was excited to work with me. As we began the coaching process, I asked her what her clients say about her—an important step in defining one's MOJO. She told me in an off-handed way that her clients say she is "intuitive" and that her massage is "different."

I knew she had been trained extensively in anatomy, physiology, and traditional medical and sports massage techniques. However, as she was learning massage, she also became interested in the concept of energy healing and became a Reiki Master (Reiki is a Japanese hands-on healing technique) so as to add to her healing tool kit. She also learned about Chinese medical modalities like acupressure, energy meridians, and emotions that are related to the functioning of our organs.

I decided that I needed to experience just what her clients were speaking of since it seemed hard for Carolyn to articulate, so I asked her to give me a massage. The very first place Carolyn put her hands was on my lower back and hips, in the exact spot where I was experiencing pain. Since I teach classes on intuitive development, I was very curious how she knew to go there first. She simply said, "Your body told me where to go." Um, what? My body told you?

She proceeded to "allow her hands to be guided" to all the spots on my body that had previous injuries or where tension was being held. Carolyn could tell which spots on my body had been injured and healed in the past, and which areas of my body were now experiencing pain or discomfort. I could feel something interesting happening in my torso when she had her hands hovering above my body when she was "balancing my chakras," and a huge presence that felt loving and helpful that she described as her healing guide and the angels. This was not your run-of-the-mill massage!

My head was spinning and my body was buzzing when I got up from her table. Never had I experienced someone so adept at working with energy, so compassionate in her manner, and so amazing with her accuracy in detecting where my body needed attention.

When I brought all of this to her attention, she

honestly had NO IDEA that these skills were her unique MOJO potion. Carolyn had seen spirits and angels since childhood—she just didn't think much of it since her talents felt natural and like "no big deal" to her. I immediately disabused her of that silly notion and said, "You are amazing!!! Why aren't you marketing yourself as a psychic massage therapist?"

Carolyn humbly responded that she didn't know that she what she did was special. Working with angels, healing guides, and intuition is so intrinsic to who Carolyn is that it didn't ever cross her mind that maybe other people would be interested in her particular skill set and that she should be leading with that.

It is not an overstatement to say that the idea of branding herself as a psychic was terrifying to her. Carolyn came from a corporate background working in human resources for high tech companies—not a lot of "woo woo" there, to say the least. She came from a traditional family; her mother was a nurse and her father and brother were both respiratory therapists. Carolyn was afraid her mother would be horrified with a psychic daughter and that she'd lose her credibility with her patients. It had already been a big enough leap to go from the corporate world to massage therapy, since her biggest fear was that people might think she was a "happy ending" masseuse working in a janky massage parlor. Jumping into "psychic" territory was just too much.

We did a lot of work together to help Carolyn ease into

becoming more vocal about her special gifts. She could hardly believe me when I told her that there were tons of people looking for someone like her. Who wouldn't want a psychic massage therapist? She baby-stepped her way into owning her MOJO by introducing herself as a "psychic muscle therapist" at networking meetings. She was very relieved that no one burned her at the stake for such an assertion, and was pleasantly surprised when people actually came up to her after the meetings and asked for her card.

After boldly owning her traditional and non-traditional healing gifts, Carolyn went on to bridge the East and West for more clients than she knew what to do with. Her massage therapy practice exploded once she claimed her magical MOJO and unapologetically put herself out there.

People who were looking for her skill set could easily find her, and the very few existing clients who weren't interested dropped off. Carolyn was astounded to find that the vast majority of her clients were thrilled to know she was capable of so many modalities and that they were in such educated, talented, and caring hands.

By coming out of the closet with her gifts, Carolyn has created a business that serves her community's health and wellbeing and benefits her and her family with more financial abundance than she could have ever guessed. I appreciate her skill so much that Carolyn and I now partner together to do healing work on clients that mixes energy work/chakra reading/coaching and a whole lotta other cool stuff that we call "Healing MOJO." These sessions have become some of the most rewarding and thrilling work we've ever done!

Scads of clients wanted Carolyn's MOJO and were more than willing to pay for it. They are literally flocking to her and are willing to wait weeks to get an appointment! All for something that she had taken for granted and had been too nervous to put out there. I promise you, dear reader, people want your MOJO too.

Chapter 6:
MOJO and Your Intuition

"You have to leave the city of your comfort and go into the wilderness of your intuition. You can't get there by bus, only by hard work and risk and by not quite knowing what you're doing, but what you'll discover will be wonderful. What you'll discover will be yourself." ~ Alan Alda

Much of what I do as a MOJO whisperer is help my clients connect to and trust their intuition. Intuition is a vital component of your MOJO. Knowing how to connect to your intuition is such an important skill because your intuition is your greatest untapped resource—it's the language of your soul!

When you learn how to trust your intuition, you learn how to trust yourself. It's that simple. And what could be more important than that? Being able to feel what is best for you down to your bones is something everyone can master.

How Does Intuition Work?

Intuition whispers to us, it doesn't shout. It comes in a complete package, like a download of thoughts or feelings. Intuition speaks softly but carries a big stick. How many times have you known intuitively that what you were doing was the wrong move yet done it anyway, only to later be proved right? It's maddening when we don't listen to the guidance that is inherent in our being.

When we continually ignore our intuition, the results are everywhere we look—a shitty job, abusive or draining relationships, unfulfilled goals, poor health, or money problems. Your intuitively-connected self knows exactly what's wrong with your life, but your rational, logical brain doesn't always want to listen. We don't change what sucks because change is hard, and most of us don't like it. Which is why we stay, comfortably uncomfortable, where it feels safe—even if it's miserable. We crave certainty, and to the unsure person, intuition feels peripheral.

The reason we don't listen is because the temporal lobe of our brain censors intuitive information. It's a nay-sayer to any information that doesn't come with proof. Listening to that censor is like listening to an annoying talk radio host who shoots down any ideas that weren't his own. It comes across as doubt, rationalizing, or the urge to placate. But as you've no doubt heard many times, going with your gut can save your life.

Learning to Listen to My Intuition

Right before I became a life coach, my life was at a stressful crossroads personally and professionally. I was working as a substitute teacher at my children's school because the hours worked for my family. My husband traveled frequently for his job in high tech, and I was the primary caretaker for our boys. My youngest son had learning issues that hadn't yet been diagnosed, and I was desperate to find a way to help him in school. I thought if I worked at school, I could protect him from bullies who made fun of him because of his learning difficulties, while observing other kids' learning styles and challenges for clues to what might be going on with my son. I hoped that if I was at school, my son would feel safer and happier, and that maybe I could figure out what was going on with him so that we could get him the help he needed.

It worked—a teacher I worked with told me about a developmental pediatrician in our area who diagnosed learning disabilities, and she was an absolute godsend. My son began to learn more easily and to like school more once we knew what we were dealing with.

I stayed at my teaching job a couple years longer than necessary, mostly because it was close and convenient. My husband, Alex, thought it would be great if I became a full-time teacher, since I had the experience and the administration and students liked me there. Those things were all true, but I knew it wasn't what I wanted.

My husband saw me struggling with my "life purpose" and thought becoming a full-time teacher was the next logical step in my career path. And it was the next logical step—it was just not the step that felt right to me.

Listening to the Signs

I dragged my feet and stubbornly procrastinated when it came to anything that had to do with becoming a full-time teacher. I was actually hoping I would be turned down for the teacher credential program. I wasn't. I hoped I would fail the entrance exam. I didn't. I passed my test with flying colors and was accepted with open arms to the program.

This all looked like success, right? So why did I feel so sick to my stomach? Why did it feel like I was moving through quicksand to accomplish anything related to my new logical career path? Alex asked me daily for a couple of months if I had sent in my payment for the credential program. We would argue about why I hadn't sent it, and I would end up crying and saying I didn't want to go through with it. Alex was exasperated with my lack of action and he felt the pressure of being a year away from paying college tuition for our oldest son with my financial contribution being puny at best. He thought having a safe teaching job with benefits was the sure bet, and that I would like it once I got past my initial hesitation. It got so contentious that I was actually afraid my husband would leave me if I didn't go into the program.

I had never felt so stuck in my entire life. I cannot overstate how lost I felt—completely MOJO-less. I was absolutely miserable, and I walked around with a perpetual knot in my stomach and lump in my throat. The problem was that I knew I didn't want to be a teacher, but I didn't know what I wanted to do instead. I was praying and begging the Universe to help me. "Give me a sign!" I begged.

When my friend Cyndi asked me to go to Oprah's *O You!* conference that I spoke about earlier, I nearly didn't go. I was very excited about attending (my intuition speaking to me), but I started talking myself out of going because I was afraid it was frivolous and self-indulgent (my dumb rational brain finding fault with the Universe's spectacular plan.) I felt so worthless that I didn't think I could justify spending $79 for the ticket.

I'm so grateful that I listened to my excitement rather than my doubt, because that conference changed my life. Learning about life coach training was exactly what I needed to hear at exactly the right moment. Investigating the details of what the life coaching training program entailed and what it covered, and seeing a clear path to how I could make it work gave me a sense of excitement and purpose that I utterly lacked when thinking about teaching.

When I looked at the cost of the life coach training, it was the EXACT SAME amount of money as getting my teaching credential. Pushing the "Pay Now" button felt easy when it was to learn how to be a life coach, whereas paying to enter the teaching credential program had felt like the most difficult thing I could possibly do.

Here's the deal: I needed to be willing to lose my security to gain myself. It may sound dramatic, but it's true. I felt I would be killing a piece of my soul I'd never get back if I went down the teaching track. If I had taken the safe road that was making me sick, I would not be writing this book right now!

The procrastination, the pain in my stomach, the lump in my throat, and the tears were all signs that I wasn't listening to my intuition. The Universe had a plan for me, but the message was to be received at the conference—which was why I had felt I couldn't send the check for the teaching credential. The stuck feeling indicated that my head wanted one thing (to please my husband and make some college money) but my heart wanted another (to fulfill my destiny as the MOJO whisperer!)

Becoming a coach felt scary, but exciting and strangely "right." It made sense, and everything I had experienced up to the moment I made that choice felt necessary to get me to where I needed to be. I knew what it felt like to be stuck and ashamed at my lack of direction. Sometimes I think I endured that experience just so I could tell that story to clients who are in the midst of some variation of my very own story. It helps them trust me because they know I've been through it, and my happy outcome seems to give them hope.

Listening to Your Intuition

When the logical, safe road feels sickening and soul-killing, listen. If your marriage is suffocating, yet somehow you think you must tolerate it, listen. If your job is paying the bills, but on Sunday afternoon you begin to dread Monday morning, listen. It doesn't have to be this way.

But following your intuition doesn't always mean making huge life shifts (though sometimes it certainly does). Sometimes it just means making small adjustments. My friend Chellie Kammermeyer followed her MOJO into working as a Reiki Master, but after a while became a little bored with just giving energy healing treatments. But when she became focused on teaching others what she knew, she felt completely fulfilled—and that excitement bled over into her one-on-one work as well. Chellie wasn't in the wrong business, she just needed a tweak. Now her mantra is "a healer in every home," and she is well on her way to single-handedly making that a reality!

Your intuition is never hostile or bullying. It has a kind and neutral quality. It feels like a gentle hand on your back, guiding you to the best outcome. When you learn to tune in to the language of your soul, you will be led to the right answer—even to your highest calling. And you will definitely be guided to help you identify your Magical, Original, Joyful Offering to the world!

I teach an intuitive development program with my good friend and amazing intuitive coach Mary Welty-Dapkus called "The Intuitive Gym" in which we help people learn to listen to their instincts. In fact, Mary was the person who identified my capacity for empathy as one of my superpowers. It turns out that one aspect of Mary's magical MOJO is identifying HOW her clients are intuitive, because she says it's one of the ways we are smart.

Do you see intuitive information in your mind's eye or with your actual peepers? That's clairvoyance. Hear information as a thought that someone is speaking to you? That's clairaudience. Feel other people's feelings in your own body or feel viscerally whether a situation feels good or bad? Clairsentience. Experience a burst of knowing so quickly that you can't figure out HOW you know what you know? Claircognizance. Touch someone or something and get "vibes" that give you information? That's psychometry. I had no idea I was picking up information intuitively through any of these senses that match up with our actual five senses until I met Mary, but once I did—my intuitive MOJO went through the roof! Incidentally, Mary had no idea that her talent for spotting one's "intuitive how" was special! That sneaky MOJO.

MOJO in Motion...

One of the exercises our students have great success with is keeping an intuition notebook. To keep an intuition notebook, just record every little intuitive nudge you feel and write it down (or keep it in the notes section of your phone). Then go back later and write if it was correct or off base.

For example:
- If you were reluctant to go to the new greasy spoon in town, but caved to the desires of your buddies—and then you got a wicked case of food poisoning—that was your intuition speaking to you.
- Any time you say "I KNEW that was going to happen!"—write it down.
- If you see a picture in your head of a lost item in a certain place, go look for it there! Your intuition may be giving you a clue. Did you find it? Write it down.

Try to notice HOW you perceived that information. Was it through touching something, hearing something, seeing something, feeling something, or just knowing something? You'll begin to notice you have a proclivity towards a couple of these ways of intuiting information, and once you know how you receive it, you will trust it more. Every time you confirm an intuitive "hit," it gives your logical brain proof that you can listen to your instincts. In time, the mind chatter that says your instincts are stupid or baseless will become quieter and you will be better able to hear (and trust) your intuitive voice.

Chapter 7:
Preamble to MOJO Killers

"Everything you want is on the other side of fear."
~ Jack Canfield

Now that you know your MOJO is your Magical, Original, Joyful Offering to the world, I want to put a spotlight on the MOJO assassins in your life that you might not be aware of. These MOJO killers are hiding in plain sight—just waiting to crush your swagger and turn you into a soulless drone.

Let me spell it out in the most basic way: **FEAR is fucking up your MOJO**. I expound upon the specific ways your MOJO is getting stuck in the following chapters, but I want to be very clear that, at its most elementary level, each MOJO killer is fear of one sort or another.

- *Mistake-o-phobia* is the fear of screwing up.
- *Compare and Despair* is the fear of not being or having enough.

- *Conformity* is the fear of being different.
- *Analysis Paralysis* is the fear of making the wrong decision.
- *Settling* is the fear that you don't deserve more.
- *Selling Out* is being afraid that other people won't recognize your worth.
- *Turtle Shell Syndrome* is the fear of standing out and being seen in all your glory.
- *Darth Vader Heart* is the fear of having your heart broken—again.
- *Cynicism* is the fear of having your hopes dashed.
- *Slothiness* is the fear of moving forward.
- *All Work and No Play* is the fear that having fun will block your success.
- *Stage Fright* is performance anxiety—the fear of not being perfect when it's your time to shine.
- *Hanging out with Energy Vampires* stems from the "disease to please"—fear that your only worth in a relationship is based on how well you meet someone else's needs.
- *Having Friends in Low Places* is the fear of being alone.

Common Fears

So many things keep us small, scared, and stifled. We fear the unknown because we are terrified we won't know how to deal with a new reality. We fear change because we are afraid we won't know how to navigate uncharted waters. We fear being rejected because it brings up our fears of unworthiness. We fear poverty because we fear being powerless. We fear our own power the most, because we are afraid to be 100% conscious and responsible for everything we do. Having nothing and no one to blame puts the ball in our court, and sometimes we are scared to take the shot.

The Reptilian Brain

Did you know you have a neural structure wrapped around your brain stem that scientists call "the reptilian brain"? This part of the brain is responsible for the fight, flight, or freeze instinct. Its sole purpose is to keep you safe by screaming bloody murder about possible dangers day and night. When a thug challenges you for domination of your cave, you fight. When being chased by a T-Rex—you take flight. If you can't do either, you might just have to freeze and pray the threat passes. All of these instincts are vital to our survival—if we live in a jungle (or a shopping mall on Black Friday).

Apparently the reptile brain gets a little bored with our lives in the 21st century—since it's got a job to do, dammit!—so it sends us signals that we need to be very afraid not only when we are in actual mortal danger, but whenever we sense any kind of what Martha Beck calls "lack or attack"—so even when things are going great, your inner mind lizard may shriek that your good fortune can't last for long! *What kind of fuckery is this?*

Our entire lives are flooded with fears about not having enough, being enough, doing enough—lack, lack, and more lack. When not feeling like a filthy scumbag for having fears of lack, we are deluged with thoughts of people trying to hurt us physically or emotionally. Just learning that this fear-based reptilian brain exists gives my clients peace, knowing that they are not alone or crazy for having these incessant anxious thought ramblings. The awareness alone can help you to consciously turn the volume down on your mind's screeching once you know that it's coming from a twitchy little gecko!

Feel the Pain

Here's the deal—every problem we encounter comes from attempting to avoid pain. We will do ANYTHING to not feel pain. We will use eating, drinking, drugs, shopping, having sex, overworking, gambling, video gaming, internet surfing, denial, or any variety of escapism to numb ourselves to the pain we feel. Pretending we are not in pain is a skill we learn very early on in our socialization. Acknowledging, sitting with, and feeling our pain until it dissipates is not.

But we should be learning those skills, because if we felt more able to cope with painful feelings, we wouldn't be running from our truth like we are on fire. Not being true to yourself is murdering your MOJO, because authenticity is your MOJO's foundation. The real you—warts and all—is where your MOJO lives.

When doubt rears its ugly head, you'll know it because you will fall down the rabbit hole into the land of "what if." What if I leave my husband and I'm alone for the rest of my life? What if I go back to school and I'm the oldest one there and I can't keep up? What if I ask my friend to stop putting me down and she abandons me? What if I leave my crappy job and I can't get another one and then I end up living in a cardboard box or in a van down by the river? If we are going to escape the land of "what if," we must follow the what-if scenarios all the way through.

I had a lovely client whom I will call Bob. He had a nasty little habit of fretting over imagined financial ruin whenever he felt insecure. I challenged his fear by asking him to play the "what if " game all the way through to the end. Here's how our conversation went:

> *Me: What would happen if you lost all your money?*
> *Bob: I guess I'd sell my house.*
> *Me: Do you have equity in your house?*
> *Bob: Yes, it would be enough money to last me for a couple of years.*
> *Me: OK, well what if you don't get a new job and you plow through all your money?*
> *Bob: Why wouldn't I get a new job?*
> *Me: I don't know, maybe you suffer a traumatic brain injury and you can't remember your name, let alone any of the skills you get paid to use now.*
> *Bob: Um, I guess my wife would make money? Or*

I could live with one of my kids?

Me: Well what if everyone abandons you? Then what would you do?

Bob: That wouldn't happen, I've been happily married for thirty-two years, and my kids love me.

Me: But what if they did, then what would you do? (Can you see how annoying I am?)

Bob: I have friends, and I could get disability?

Me: And you still aren't homeless?

Bob: OK, I see where you're going with this. No, I'm not homeless. I guess the worst thing that could happen to me is that I live in a trailer.

Me: So the absolute worst thing that could happen to you is that you live in a trailer? Seriously? Are you still married?

Bob: Well... yeah.

Me: So you live in a trailer with the woman you love. That's the worst thing that could happen to you? But are you eating cat food...?

And so it goes. Bob had spent so much time gnashing his teeth and wringing his hands about imagined financial ruin...and his worst-case scenario is living in a trailer with his beloved wife of thirty-two years. Which, by the way, is better than most of the world lives. It seems funny or exaggerated when we play the "what if" game all the way through, but until we question its assumptions our rational brain truly has us looking over our shoulder, perpetually waiting for the other shoe to drop, and predicting catastrophe. That's just sad.

Since homelessness is such a pervasive fear, and a great example for the "what-if" game, please indulge me here in breaking it down. Homelessness doesn't usually doesn't just sneak up on you. It means you are unable to get another job, you don't have any money saved up, you have no friends or family to help you, you have nothing to sell to make money, you receive no aid from the government, and that you've been physically kicked out of your home, which usually takes months if not years depending on your circumstance. In other words, homelessness usually is a last step in a string of very unfortunate events, not the first step. You are a resourceful person, you have time to recover! But until you help your rational brain realize that, it will have you feeling like you're constantly on the edge of disaster. We gotta unfuck that shit.

This applies whether your fear is homelessness, loss of relationships, or some other scary scenario your particular brain likes to torture you with. So the next time you find yourself asking "what if" because you are borrowing trouble from the future—ask yourself what the worst thing that could happen would be. Then follow the "what if" trail all the way through. Remember that you are a resilient MOJO-maker and you can create a better circumstance. Just use your resources and keep the faith! Remember, worrying is just a prayer for what we DON'T want. Use the power of visualization for good, not evil. Worrying is not a sustainable or helpful barrier against suffering. It creates suffering. Don't feed the beast!

Let's look under all the rocks and find the creepy crawlies that are sucking the MOJO out of our lives, and then unleash the antidotes. As the saying goes, FEAR is **F**alse **E**vidence **A**ppearing **R**eal. We can conquer the world once we know what's holding us back. Come on, grab your cape and your boots—let's roll!

Chapter 8:

MOJO Killer #1
Mistake-o-Phobia

"Anyone who has never made a mistake has
never tried anything new."
~ Albert Einstein

Who hasn't felt the fear of screwing up and allowed that to stop them from a new endeavor? Can you imagine how much promise has gone unfulfilled because of the fear of putting ourselves out there?

How many artists keep their work in closets for fear of not being good enough? How many athletes are afraid to try out for the team? How many relationships have been prematurely nipped in the bud for fear of failure? How many people have held themselves back from the perfect job because they were afraid to apply? How many business ideas go up in smoke for fear of taking a risk?

It's a tragedy that so many of us are more afraid of making a mistake than we are of never reaching our potential. My mission in life is to inspire all those who are on the verge of stepping into the light to have the courage to leap! You have greatness inside of you. Don't allow mistake-o-phobia to rob you of your MOJO!

Accept It—You're Human Too

There are no perfect people, and you can be sure that whomever you look up to has made plenty of blunders on their path to greatness. Imperfection is part of the deal of being human, I'm afraid—and this may seem obvious, but mistake-o-phobia is the number one reason people lose their MOJO.

Even rock stars make mistakes—they sing a flat note or may forget the words altogether. I've seen Beyoncé fall flat on her face during a dance routine, and then pop up and swagger on as if nothing happened. Even with all the hours of practice in the world, the best of us can (and will) make embarrassing mistakes. It's not that we're stupid, ill-prepared, or foolish in any way— we're just human beings subject to the laws of gravity or momentary memory lapse. What makes for a great show is when a performer acknowledges the slip-up and makes a joke out of it. The audience rallies behind their hero and urges them on.

I once saw a speaker forget her train of thought. Instead of stretching out the moment uncomfortably and stalling until she could find the words, she put her hands up to her mouth and burst out laughing. She said "Oh my gosh, I totally forgot what I was saying—I think it's the menopause!" The audience laughed with her and reminded her of where she was, and she just giggled and got back on track. It was one of the most endearing things I've ever seen and it actually made the audience LOVE her. Her authenticity was so inspiring and guileless. She gained credibility and scored a whole new pack of fans. Being human is appealing, being a robot is not.

We all have technical difficulties in life. Maybe you sent out an important email with a few typos, or made an accounting error that is a pain in the ass to fix. The important thing is: How did you recover? Did you hide from your mistake as if it never happened and hope no one found out? Bad move. Covering your tracks rarely works because truth has a way of rising to the surface. Most of the time, the lie that covers the mistake is more unforgivable than the original faux pas.

The antidote to mistake-o-phobia is transparency. Telling the truth can be quite freeing for ourselves and is positively intoxicating to witness in others.

How to Recover from a Mistake:
Lessons from *Scandal*.

It's like the TV show *Scandal*. What does Olivia Pope always have her clients do when there is proof of their guilt? She tells them to come clean. Had an affair with the handyman and there are pictures? **Come clean**.

Running for the Democratic nomination for

president and had a baby at fifteen that your mom raised as your sister and the other side is going to expose you? **Come clean**.

Stole a memory card from your boyfriend the district attorney's safe that proves the last presidential election was rigged? **Come clean**, apologize profusely and sincerely, and attempt to make amends.

Whining or blaming others only makes you look worse and keeps the scandal on the front page.

Thankfully, most of us aren't running to become Commander in Chief—so there's considerably less attention on us. But when you're out there doing your thing, whatever that is, the fear of making a mistake is an instant MOJO deflator.

Other people can forgive a lot of misdeeds when we take responsibility for our behavior and really own it. It's hard to hold a grudge when someone says "Yup, I really blew it big time on that one—I'm really sorry." You gotta own your fugly!

Try, Try, Try

Pink had it right—you gotta get up and try, try, try.

What's worse than making a mistake in the middle of a mission is never attempting the mission at all. Being awesome is your mission. It's getting out of your own way and doing the damn thing you said you wanted to do. Remember, most people *want* you to be awesome. They are cheering for you, wishing you well, wanting you to succeed. Those who have a nasty agenda based on jealousy or ugliness will just have to suck it. (I'll talk more about that in Turtle Shell Syndrome.)

Do The Work

Most of the time, our fears are caused by thoughts we're having that we are just automatically believing without even stopping to question whether or not they're true. The next time you find yourself in a fearful place, try to identify the particular thought that is distressing you, and ask yourself these questions from spiritual teacher Byron Katie. Her method of inquiry is called "The Work™," and it's about overcoming painful thoughts that keep you stuck.

1. Is it true?
2. Can you absolutely know that it's true?
3. How do you react when you think that thought?
4. Who would you be without the thought?

And then, turn it around.

Example of a painful thought:
   "If I quit my shitty job everyone will think I'm a failure."

1. Is it true? How do you know everyone will think you are a failure?
2. Can you absolutely know that it's true? Have you really asked every single person you know

(everyone) if they will think you are a failure if you quit your shitty job?

3. How do you react when you think that thought? I stay stuck in a shitty job and feel like crap, and shame myself for not having the courage to move. I overeat (or spend too much money, or drink too many glasses of wine) because I'm stressed out and need to "treat" myself. I snap at my kids because I'm miserable. I tell myself there are no better jobs out there and I should just be grateful for the one I have, yada yada yada. Basically you think crap thoughts that lead to you feeling crappy.

4. Who would you be without the thought? If I were magically no longer physically able to think the thought that everyone would think I was a failure if I quit my shitty job, I guess I wouldn't have any fear. I also wouldn't be able to blame other people for holding me back from moving on.

Turn That Thought Around

After asking the questions and listening deeply to the answers, the next step in The Work™ is finding what are called "turnarounds." To make a turnaround, you look for several opposites or variations of your original painful thought. So, turnarounds for this thought might be, "If I *don't* quit my shitty job, everyone will think I'm a failure," "If I don't quit my shitty job, *I* will think I'm a failure," or "If I quit my shitty job, everyone will think I'm brave."

You can get really creative with the turnarounds! Let your mind stretch here. You can even play with the wording and come up with variations like, "What other people think of me is none of my business, so I better be happy with what I think of me—and in this case, I will be happy with me if I ditch my shitty job."

Pick the thought that feels better to you than the original thought, but also doesn't feel like you are lying to yourself. It should feel lighter, but not completely delusional.

Next, can you think of an example or two of how these turnarounds just might be as true or truer than your original, painful thought? For example, can you think of at least one person who would be cheering your bravery if you took a chance on a new job? Once your mind can see an example of how the painful thought might not actually be 100% true, it starts to loosen its grip on fear a bit and open to new possibilities.

MOJO in Motion...

Now you try. Write a crappy thought here...

_____

_____

1) Is it true?

_____

2) Is it _really_ true?

_____

3) How do you treat yourself when you think that thought?

_____

4) Who would you be without that thought?

_____

Now turn it around into a thought that feels better, but not delusional...

_____

Notice how much relief you feel when you can choose a better-feeling thought!

Chapter 9:
MOJO Killer #2
Compare and Despair

"Comparison is the thief of joy."
~ Theodore Roosevelt

Do you constantly compare yourself to others and then despair about what you lack?

Do you think that whatever someone else has is probably better than yours? Or that other people are happier, taller, thinner, smarter, funnier, better looking, cooler, richer, or have more friends than you?

The Grass Is Always Greener

Maybe they live in a better neighborhood, or go on more vacations. Or they have more toys, or a better career, or more successful kids. The grass is always greener on the other side, blah blah blah....But here's the funny thing about that. Someone you know is thinking the very same thing about you!

Compare and despair is a MOJO robber. It takes you out of the present moment and plays on your insecurities so that you are constantly waiting to feel better *someday*— when the planets are all aligned correctly, or when you get pregnant, or when your kids are more independent, or when you lose thirty pounds, or when you quit that crappy job. It's like waiting for your life to begin instead of actually living it! At the risk of sounding like Dr. Phil, someday is not a day of the week, people! The clock is ticking, and this is not a dress rehearsal.

"Costco Cart Syndrome"

We all have momentary lapses of sanity in which we covet other people's stuff. I call it "Costco cart syndrome". Whenever I go to Costco I find myself drawn to what someone else may have in their cart, and for some reason I usually think it's better than what I have in my cart. Usually what happens is that I realize about three seconds later that I have that same thing that looks better *in my very own cart*. What the hell is that about?

It's the fear of missing out on something else, then comparing what you've got and then despairing about your feeling screwed out of said amazing thing.

Get Off the Crazy Train

Can you see how this is the crazy train to nowhere? Women are entering plastic surgeons' offices with requests for Angelina Jolie's lips, Kim Kardashian's butt, or some Playboy model's boobs. Or we may want to be taller or shorter, for our skin to be lighter or darker, hair curlier or straighter, blonder or more brunette—it's never-ending. What is all this about? Why the constant dissatisfaction with what we have and where (or who) we are?

Nowhere is this phenomenon more apparent than on social media. I know many people who have left Facebook because they cannot stand the comparison of the virtual lives of their "friends" to their own actual lives. To look at some people's social media personas, life looks like one big vacation/pedicured toes in the sand/cocktail party/night on the town.

Everyone's kid is "amazing" and "special," and by the looks of things is simultaneously maintaining a 4.8 GPA/ playing football on a scholarship for Stanford/a violin virtuoso/most popular/single-handedly brokering world peace…and feeding the homeless while doing modeling on the side for Abercrombie and Fitch.

I hear a lot of comparing and despairing over how "other" people are so much further along in their careers—wayyyy further than they are. As a coach I am a member of several Facebook forums for coaches, and sometimes the hype is overwhelming. It looks like one long stream of "OMG I'm leading a retreat in Maui/speaking at the UN/conferring with members of Congress/on retainer for movie stars/writing my next book/making $30K a day for speaking to corporations." It can make me feel like whatever I'm doing just plain sucks in comparison. Compare and despair is a BITCH!

But here's the thing—none of these coaches are doing all of these things put together. They may be doing one or two, but I've amalgamated all of this amazingness into one person we can not-so affectionately call "everybody."

The truth is "everybody" is not living this life—and if I'm looking at each coach's individual super-cool accomplishments and lumping them all together, I'm starting a shit spiral that is not based in any sort of reality.

Your Everybody and Your Jedi Council

Martha Beck has a great tool called "Who's Your Everybody?" She has you write down six actual people who in your mind constitute your *everybody*. Usually there's at least one parent, a spouse, sibling, teacher, boss, or friend. We were taught to use this tool when a client says things like, "*Everybody* wants me to get my master's degree, but I really want to sell everything and become a scuba instructor in Fiji." When listening to your *everybody* is keeping you stuck or small, just look at who you are actually thinking of when you say that.

If an individual's contribution to your thoughts feels stifling, then you are probably seeing life through their lens, with their sensibilities. Again, ask yourself: would you like to run your life the way this person runs theirs? If the thought of that makes your blood run cold, consider kicking this person out of your peanut gallery and forming a new advisory board you can look to—what author and entrepreneur coach Pamela Slim calls a "Jedi Council." She advises us to create a mental consortium of leadership, which can include people you know personally or don't, living or deceased. The only requirement is that you believe each member of your Jedi Council to be admirable and wise—someone you deeply respect and see as a symbol of who you want to be when you grow up! And then let them, rather than your less-than-supportive "everybody," influence your decisions.

Kicking "Everybody" to the Curb and Assembling Your Jedi Council

Imagine that you have the guidance of every great leader with an impeccable moral compass to go to for advice. Who would you pick? I'm going for the big guns—how 'bout Gandhi, Abraham Lincoln, Mother Teresa, Buddha, and even Jesus for big philosophical or moral questions?

Mojo In Motion...

For business advice I might go to Steve Jobs, Warren Buffett, Sir Richard Branson, or Russell Simmons. For personal growth, some of my heroes are Oprah, Martha Beck, Marianne Williamson, Tony Robbins, and Eckhart Tolle. Pick a teacher, friend, mentor or family member who has always been encouraging and given you good guidance. Replace your negative "everybody" voices with your very own hand-picked all-star steering committee!

Who's Your Everybody?

List six actual people that comprise your version of *everybody*:

1)_____

2)_____

3)_____

4)_____

5)_____

Now that you see who you've unconsciously been letting run your life and possibly making you feel bad about yourself, you can make a conscious decision to stop listening to their (mostly imaginary!) judgments. Turn to your Jedi Council instead!

Make Your Own Jedi Council

Who are six people (famous or not) you admire, respect, and would happily take guidance from?

1)_____

2)_____

3)_____

4)_____

5)_____

6)_____

The antidote for compare and despair is counting your blessings! Start with where you are right NOW. Look at what you DO have going for you and begin to feel gratitude for it.

What am I proud of right now?
List five things here…

1)_____

2)_____

3)_____

4)_____

5)_____

How am I unique and fabulous?

1)_____

2)_____

3)_____

4)_____

5)_____

Five things I am grateful for right now are...

1)_____

2)_____

3)_____

4)_____

5) _____

Chapter 10:
MOJO Killer #3
I Wanna Be Like You!

"It is better to fail in originality than to succeed in imitation."
~ Herman Melville

Ever seen an Elvis impersonator? Is there anything sadder? Nothing against impersonators in general—they can be highly entertaining—but in the real world it's just sort of pitiful. Pretending to be someone else gives you no swag. ZERO!

Did you know that Bruno Mars played an Elvis impersonator when he was four years old in a movie called *Honeymoon In Vegas?* He used to imitate Elvis in his family's band. I'm sure Bruno developed a lot of his own MOJO while studying and mimicking Elvis as a kid—but he does not impersonate Elvis NOW. He didn't become famous for doing a perfect impression of Elvis. Bruno Mars obviously studied amazing talent, and while watching him you can see the influences of

Michael Jackson and other great pop/R&B legends, but he has his own distinct MOJO. He has a great sense of humor, a love for '70s pimp wear, an amazing work ethic, incredible skill, and an individual, unique style.

The Great Pretender

You know when someone is pretending—you can feel it. It feels slimy, or pretentious, or just insincere. There's a ton of ego involved. Making believe you are someone else means that who YOU are isn't good enough. It also means that *other* people are better and more worthwhile than you are. ***That is so not true!***

Remember when the TV show *Friends* came out? Every other network rushed to get another *Friends*-esque show out immediately following its success. There were the requisite single six friends with quirky personalities, living in some urban area, being cool. But we didn't just want to see six random people being quirky and dating in a city. We wanted to see *those* six people at *that* coffee shop in *that* city. It was the characters' chemistry with one another that made *Friends* a phenomenon, not the formula.

Now, emulating someone else's characteristics or their attributes is another story—there is actually a healthy way to begin to embody swimmer Diana Nyad's tenacity, or Bill Gates' vision. Studying how someone you admire became successful is really smart. Pretending to be them is a little creepy, and it actually sucks your own sense of personal power.

It's a little like when famous people have an entourage...the people in the entourage may think that they themselves are VIPs because the celebrity is a VIP—importance by association. But proximity to power only makes you moderately powerful while you are with the VIP. Authentic power comes from being true to yourself. Unique is muy MOJO! Standing in your own power is mucho MOJO!

Copying Someone Else's MOJO Is No Bueno.

Being a chameleon is a great survival technique, but it's a lousy road to MOJO. Trust me, I've done it—badly. In a high school talent show, I got ripped to shreds by one particular judge for singing not one, but two vintage Barbra Streisand songs—and for doing my very best Babs impression.

During college, I had a summer job as a receptionist at a commercial real estate company. The previous receptionist was much loved and highly over-qualified for that job. She was being moved up and I was taking her place. I was inexperienced and intimidated. How would I ever compare to this grown woman who had effortlessly mastered the hub of the office? I couldn't, but oh how I tried! So I answered the phone like I had stolen her identity—I copied her tone, her pace, her accent, and her laugh. I was a twenty-year-old '80s valley girl pretending to be a forty-year-old Southern belle.

How sad! I wish I could say I was done copycatting in my twenties, but au contraire, mon frère. Years later, I worked as a teacher's aide for the second-grade teaching team at my son's elementary school. Sometimes the teacher I was helping out that day would ask me to teach a lesson or lead a group. I found myself copying each teacher's style right down to the hand gestures she used, volume of her voice, cadence of her speech, and the cues that she used to keep the kids' attention.

It wasn't until I became a fill-in teacher at that school that I created my very own style of teaching. When I finally had the confidence in myself and my way of doing things, I became a very good teacher. I'd finally come into my own. I found my own teaching MOJO!

Learn from the Greats, Then Make it Your Own

WHY do we feel compelled to copy greatness? Well, some reasons are really good. In art school, students are asked to replicate famous works so as to improve upon their technique. Learning from masters is a great step to cultivating your own MOJO. It's also great to know what is considered top of the line in your own industry or in an area of interest for you.

But it's also important to learn about the outliers, those who are successful because they didn't follow the rules or conform to standards deemed appropriate by authorities. What's good for your MOJO is to study the greats, learn from their technique and then MAKE IT YOUR OWN. As the famous saying goes, "Be yourself; everyone else is already taken. "

The antidote to conformity is individuality. Americans are famous for rugged individualism. We are a nation of innovators, and innovation is the future, baby. Other nations may be famous for pirating or copying American inventions, but American culture fosters entrepreneurship and originality. We are encouraged to open businesses and work for ourselves—something that many immigrants are attracted to the promise of. It takes courage not to jump on the bandwagon or to un-follow the pack. However, that's where all of the payoff is, and it's the piece that's missing for most people I coach who are feeling stifled in their lives. They have lost their spunk and individuality and replaced that feeling with being a cog in the wheel. Shuffling off to a soulless job where you need to follow ridiculous protocols and you feel devoid of personal power is the fast track to MOJOlessness. Don't let this be you!

MOJO in Motion...

Where are you stuck in someone else's brand of MOJO?

_____

Why are you doing that?

_____

What do you have to do to free yourself of someone else's persona and do things your own way?

_____

Now, take a few minutes to figure out what you like in other people's MOJO. What is it that appeals to you?

_____

Chapter 11:

MOJO Killer #4
Analysis Paralysis

"We are dying from overthinking. We are slowly killing ourselves by thinking about everything. Think. Think. Think. You can never trust the human mind anyway. It's a death trap."

~ Anthony Hopkins

When you are presented with too many choices, your brain goes haywire. In this information age we are constantly deluged with choices to make. Which emails should you delete and how should you respond to the plethora of messages requiring a response? Which toothpaste should you buy when there's eighty-seven different kinds of on the shelf? Which type of lemon drop martinis should you make for your party when there are thirty-four recipes online? Which charities are best to support when there is so much need? Which TV shows do you choose to watch or music stations to listen to when there are thousands of choices? Out of hundreds of thousands of options, which books or articles do you read when you need information?

Too. Many. Choices.

How many times have you gone looking for an outfit for an important event, been overwhelmed with your choices, and just left the store with nothing? Or looked online at a slew of vacation destinations with different packages on a million different websites and gone into a dissociative fugue because you can't select just one option?

We have more choices now than ever before, and if you wanted to, you could spend your entire life researching every single permutation of every possible purchase or decision you make. It's exhausting, depleting, and murder on your MOJO.

I call this MOJO killer analysis paralysis.

MOJO Is Decisive

You see, MOJO knows what it wants—it's decisive. It doesn't hem and haw and freak out over what the best logical choice is. It doesn't do mind-numbing amounts of research to decide on the most favorable outcome.

MOJO lives life with ease and grace, not looking over its shoulder to see if a better offer is coming around the bend.

When your MOJO is working, you can be decisive and confident in the decisions you make because fear is not riding shotgun in the passenger's seat, broadcasting all the different ways you could screw this up if you don't choose wisely. What you need to do is to backhand that fear-based bitch's voice in your head and say, "Thanks so much for your input—now shut the hell up."

I'm not asking you to be impulsive—making bad, rushed decisions based on exasperation is no way to go. Just don't sweat the small stuff. And as author Richard Carlson said, *it's all small stuff.* Having a little more trust in the Universe will put you on a fast track to MOJO. Allow one choice to come to the forefront. Make it a game. Notice how no one dies when you make a bad choice about which conditioner really might heal your split ends.

The antidote to analysis paralysis is using your intuition. When you allow your intuition to guide you, your life will become easier in ways I cannot even begin to enumerate. It's as simple as allowing yourself to lie back and float rather than fighting the current. Answers that come from your intuition do not come from your logical mind. They come from a deep knowing in your gut, a little lightness in your heart, or a whisper in your ear. Intuitive impressions do not come across as bossy or derisive or self-critical. They feel affirming and light.

Watch for Synchronicity

When you really need to know something, you will get more than one chance to notice it and examine it. Begin to notice patterns. Do you keep hearing, multiple times, about this awesome podcast your friends just love? Give it a listen.

A super-great doctor who you hear the name of three times in a week? Check her out. Looking for a new job and hear from several colleagues that one particular company is hiring? It's a SIGN. The Universe speaks in synchronicities.

It's as if there's an angel on your shoulder trying to get your attention and guide you to your next endeavor. It doesn't always mean that the choice that keeps popping up is the right one, or the only right one, but I've noticed that it's at least a nod in the right direction and usually leads to another clue in the scavenger hunt of life.

Action Is Your Friend

Here's a reassuring thought—*a step in the wrong direction is better than standing still.* Why? Because once you move in the wrong direction, you'll know and you have one less path to explore. The Universe rewards movement. *The Bible* says, "God helps those who help themselves," right? Newton's first law of motion states that an object that is in motion stays in motion. Once you begin to gain momentum, a snowball of opportunity forms. You will begin to feel a gentle guiding force in your life that speaks to you when you ask it for help.

MOJO works with your gut. It whispers in its soft and reassuring way, "Go with that one, baby."

The right answer for you calls to you like a siren calls a sailor.

MOJO in Motion...

Make a list of three decisions you've been putting off.

1)_____

2)_____

3)_____

Which one is the least important? Pick that one.

Allow yourself to look at two choices.
- Which one feels the most like freedom?
- Which one feels a little lighter than the other?
- Which one has a teeny tiny sparkle of excitement that the other one doesn't have?

Pick that one.

Now act on your decision and notice how you feel.
- Did anyone become maimed or injured as a result of your choice?
- Did you lose a substantial amount of money as a result of your choice?

If your choice turned out well, use this as evidence that you can trust your intuition.

If your choice didn't turn out well, go back to the drawing board and try again. It's possible that you were mistakenly using your logical brain to make the choice out of habit.

Remember, there are very few decisions that cannot be corrected. VERY FEW. Give yourself some breathing room to make a (gasp) mistake. You'll notice you make fewer mistakes the more you give yourself permission to experiment with the concept. Really, I promise.

Chapter 12:

MOJO Killer #5
"It Is What it Is" and Other
Bullshit We Tell Ourselves

"The minute you settle for less than you deserve,
you get even less than you settled for."
~ *Maureen Dowd*

A bird in the hand is worth two in the bush—except when it's not the right bird. What if it's a puny, emaciated, sad bird that would make for a pathetic feast and you only bring it home because you didn't think you could catch anything better? Or what if it's an angry, squawking bird that bites you every time you come near it? But it's always in the neighborhood, and therefore convenient to nab.

Wouldn't it be maddening to find out that there was some other big, juicy, gorgeous, darling bird with colorful plumage that shat money out of its ass when stroked just right? There! In the bush—where you didn't have the faith to explore?

Yes, that would be very sad.

(If you ever find a bird like that, let me know, OK?)

Settling Is the Devil

Settling is when you just take what is being given to you (or whatever makes the most noise) and you decide, *why yes, I suppose this will do.*

Heard yourself say any of these things lately?

It's not THAT bad.

I guess it will have to do.

I couldn't find anything else I liked, so I ended up with this one.

He/She wouldn't normally have done that, said that, behaved that way. He/she was just tired (stressed, cranky, overworked, horny, sick, hungry, drunk, not thinking…fill in your excuse de jour here)

It doesn't happen that much.

That's just how he is. I just have to deal with it.

That's how she was raised.

She doesn't even know she's being rude!

One of these days I am going to tell him that…

As soon as I (fill in the blank), then I will be able to (blank).

They didn't mean it.

Someday it will be different—when I have more time (or money, health, kids are older, have a baby, get married, get a divorce, get a new job)

And my personal favorite...*It is what it is.*
In the movie St. Vincent, Bill Murray's character says "'It is what it is' means that you're getting screwed, and that you are going to continue to get screwed." My sentiments exactly!

Hypothetically, pretend someone finds you attractive and asks you out. There's nothing particularly wrong with him or her, but you aren't feeling ecstatic about spending time with them either. You say yes, because— "Hey, what else do I have to do?" One date leads to dating which leads to being exclusive. This leads to engagement, which leads to marriage. Then ten years go by and you realize you aren't really in love with this person. Then you wonder "Why am I not happy?"

It's because you settled. He seemed good enough at the time. You didn't want to risk being alone or dating a lot of frogs to find your Prince Charming. Maybe you never felt very empowered when looking for a mate in the first place. Perhaps you just allowed whoever was interested in you into your life, because *maybe this is all there is and maybe I won't get another chance.*

Maybe your relationship is just groovy, but it's your career that you've settled for. After college, you sorta fell into a particular field and thought you'd stay for just a year, to pay the bills. You know, just to make some money until you figured out what you really wanted to do. Then you turn around and **twenty years** have gone by and you have to ask yourself "How did I end up here? I never really chose this career. It just sort of *happened.*"

If your career is a happy accident and you love what you do—fantastic! I'm behind you all the way.

But if you are unhappy in your job, and don't know if you are qualified to do anything else, listen up: ***This is not your burning desire, it's complacency.*** Do you really want to spend the rest of your life in a job you can't stand or that bores you, that doesn't use your sharpest skills or bring you any joy or meaning? Let me answer for you—NO, no you don't.

Get a New Attitude

Now, don't go quitting your job just yet. What you've got to do is start bringing the best version of yourself to the job you have right now. Not the you who's on autopilot, just going through the motions. When you up your game in the career department, the Universe takes notice. Find a way to be more of your true self in your work. Unleash your special MOJO on even the most mundane tasks. Do the best job you can even in the least ideal circumstances. Maybe your job sucks, but you don't have to. Shake yourself out of that malaise and approach your job with a new attitude. Find something to like about it, *anything*. Then focus on it—fixate on it! Try to find as many new things to like about your job as you possibly can. Being in a better frame of mind elevates your energy, which raises your vibration—which makes you a magnet for goodness, which in this case might just be a new job!

Brought a steady stream of sunshine and unicorns to the soul-sucking hellhole that is your job, and you still hate it? Run like the wind—life is too short to do work you detest.

The antidote to settling is to expect miracles. Sound hokey? Maybe so…but you *are* a miracle. Just think of how many barriers you've overcome to get to who you are at this moment. Every day is a miracle if you choose to think of it that way. Do you believe others have a charmed life and that yours is doomed? If so, I beg you to stop that shit right now! Take those self-sabotaging spectacles off immediately and replace them with optimistic ones. You can choose your outlook on life, and decide to see it through a different lens. Instead of asking "Why me?" ask yourself "Why not me?"

I love this quote from spiritual teacher Marianne Williamson,

> *"Our deepest fear is not that we are inadequate. Our deepest fear is that we are powerful beyond measure. It is our light, not our darkness that most frightens us. We ask ourselves, Who am I to be brilliant, gorgeous, talented, fabulous? Actually, who are you not to be? You are a child of God. Your playing small does not serve the world. There is nothing enlightened about shrinking so that other people won't feel insecure around you. We are all meant to shine, as children do. We were born to make manifest the glory of God that is within us. It's not just in some of us; it's in everyone. And as we let our own light shine, we unconsciously give other people permission to do the same. As we are liberated from our own fear, our presence automatically liberates others."*

We need to adjust our expectations for our lives from the place of playing small to a place of expecting that miracles are par for the course, and that you are as deserving of everyday miracles as the next person. You must believe that you are worth it, and you must hold out for what you want.

Starting tomorrow, I want you to get excited about spending the next eight hours with your most dynamic, creative, and passionate self—even while you are doing something shitty that you hate.

It's the internal monologue you're having with yourself that we want to focus on. How can you bring more of your authentic self to the place where you spend the majority of your waking hours? You may be surprised at how your coworkers begin to see you, and what they reflect back to you. I *know* you'll be surprised at how much better you feel.

Complacency Is the Enemy

Taking charge of your thought process is an attitude adjustment and it requires discipline at first. Sooner or later, it will become a habit and you will discover that you no longer have the ability to tolerate complacency in your life any more.

Truly, think hard about whether you want to live your life with the inability to tolerate complacency because *this one shift will change your life*.

- It will change your relationships—those you've been merely tolerating will fall by the wayside.
- It will change your health—you won't just chalk pain and suffering up to "Well, I'm getting older, what can I expect?"
- It will change your career—you will find opportunities to use your favorite skills and you'll begin to find purpose in your work because you will find ways to contribute meaningfully. You will no longer be able to tolerate monotonous drudgery.
- It will change everything from your finances to your wardrobe to your television viewing habits. Your ability to endure bullshit will disappear, and your life will expand in ways you can't imagine.

MOJO in Motion...

Step One: What Are You Settling For?

What are the last five things you complained about? Write them down. Is there something there that you are making OK that really isn't?

Step Two: Why Are You Settling for It?

Are you afraid that this is all you can have?

Are you afraid to change your circumstances because you are afraid of the unknown (aka the devil you know is better than the devil you don't)?

Do you feel like this is all you deserve? Or do you feel that you made your bed and now you must lie in it?

Step 3: Do You See a Pattern?

Do you notice that you are settling in a certain area of your life—relationships, career, money, material things—or just life in general?

If you notice settling in one area, ask yourself a question. What thought goes through your mind when I say, "What am I telling myself to make this OK?" It may be a self-defeating phrase you heard from your parent or teacher.

Examples:
- *So you think you're special, huh?*
- *Life's a bitch, and then you die.*

- *Life isn't fair.*
- *You can't have everything.*
- *You're LUCKY to even HAVE a boyfriend!*
- *At least you're not alone!*
- *People like us can't expect more.*
- *This is the life you chose.*

Yuck! I am feeling sick just typing these phrases. Can you see the passivity in these statements? The victim mentality? The "WHO the HELL am I to WANT MORE?" Fuck. That. Shit.

These statements are no more than your ego shielding itself from complete defeat—the idea being that if you don't want for more than what you have, you'll never be disappointed.

Step 4: Cut the Crap

You will never be able to have more for yourself if you don't feel like you deserve it. This is a self-worth issue. Does someone else deserve to be happier, thinner, richer, more loved, more respected, or more successful than you? Why? If the answer is yes—please hire a coach! If the answer is no, you must....

Step 5: Envision What You Want

Allow yourself to imagine what it would be like to have what you want. Don't worry about how—the

AWARENESS is all you need. Focus on the opportunities that may come your way courtesy of the Universe.

Step 6: Decide That You Are WORTH It!

Use that thing that keeps you from falling over called a BACKBONE and stand up for yourself. Find small ways to assert your new attitude (like sending back the salad with the wrong dressing, or returning clothing that doesn't fit quite right) and work your way up to some bigger things (asking for a promotion, a raise, flexible hours, better treatment, friends who don't talk behind your back.)

What is the first thing you want to stop settling for?

_____

Why do you want to stop allowing it?

_____

What do you tell yourself to make it okay to settle?

_____

What can your replacement thoughts be?

_____

How will you feel when you hold out for what you really want?

_____

Leo's MOJO Story

Mortgage Broker, Reiki Master, Soul-Journeying Badass

Leo was a struggling mortgage broker who was unmotivated and demoralized. He was a great guy—a veteran, a pilot who had previously worked in banking and auto sales. Leo's wife had become a Reiki Master years before, and he was her first student guinea pig.

Energy work was not something a salt-of-the-earth kind of guy like Leo would investigate on his own. But he had undergone six back surgeries, and was scheduled for a seventh when his wife tried giving him Reiki. He was amazed with the results and over time, his back pain improved so much that he didn't need another surgery.

As his disillusionment with the mortgage business increased, his desire to find another career became overwhelming. As we worked together, I encouraged Leo to follow his curiosity in any area where he felt he lost track of time.

He shocked me by announcing that he wanted to attend a workshop given by a famous medium to try his hand at talking with the dead. It turned out that he had a talent for it! Leo realized after taking several intuitive development courses that he had a particular love for guided meditation—where he would have the most amazing spiritual experiences. He began listening to guided meditations more and more frequently. In the meantime, he also became a Reiki Master—in part to spend more time with his wife and to have fun working together.

Leo went out on a limb and began offering Reiki sessions to clients. During a session he was moved to lead his client through a sort of guided meditation that he now calls a soul journey while simultaneously giving them Reiki. The client loved the experience and Leo was amazed that he was able to "see" what the client was experiencing before they were able to verbalize it. He was anxious to try it again and again with each client that came to see him. The results were amazing—his clients felt they were able to have experiences similar to that of a shamanic journey. I had never seen Leo look so full of life or excited to go to work.

As if by magic, Leo's mortgage business picked up and became fun again once he switched firms, which came directly on the heels of his finding joy leading his clients through soul journeys. One good thing deserves another! By allowing his curiosity to lead him, Leo uncovered supernatural MOJO that fueled his passion for life and enabled him to make a living at the same time.

Chapter 13:
MOJO Killer #6
Turning Tricks

"Hollywood is a place where they'll pay you
a thousand dollars for a kiss and fifty cents for your soul."
~ Marilyn Monroe

"The saddest thing about selling out is just how cheaply
most of us do it for."
~ James Bernard Frost

Ah, the golden handcuffs. Working at a job that steals your soul no matter how good the salary, bonuses, flexible hours, or benefits are is another way to lose your MOJO. When we do something *just for the money,* we're like hookers turning tricks—and our MOJO runs for the hills. You can just feel it when it happens, both for yourself and for others—it's palpable. Any victory feels empty, devoid of meaning.

I cannot tell you how many people I've coached

who feel imprisoned by their job and think they cannot leave because "my stock options are going to vest in just four years!" or "if I stick it out six more years I'll get my pension," or "if I stay through the closedown I'll get a retention bonus." Notice how the language around this sounds like it's a prison sentence where the person needs to do time in order to get the carrot at the end of the stick. Logically it sounds crazy to pass up a payout like that, and maybe it is. But you have to look at the cost emotionally, mentally, and physically as well as the financial implications when determining if you should stay or go.

A good clue that you may be selling out in your career is if you've uttered *"it pays the bills"* ever, in your whole life. I don't mean if you are a teenager working at a burger joint to gain independence. I'm talking about when you know that you despise your job and it feels like every day you are making a deal with the devil to pay your bills, because you know exactly what you yearn to do but you:

a) Are afraid of taking a chance,
b) Are afraid of what other people will say,
c) Are afraid of financial ruin,
d) Think it will be too much work
e) Enjoy complaining about your crappy life.

Ditch Black and White Thinking— Think Shades of Gray

Here's the thing: I'm not saying you have to sell all of your belongings and take a vow of poverty to chase your dreams. NOT AT ALL. What I'm saying is that you must, and I do mean *must*, bring what you love out of the shadows and into the light of your life. Pamela Slim calls this your "side hustle"—doing the thing you love at night and on weekends while you plot your escape from the job you do not love. It's actually a terrible idea to irresponsibly quit the job that puts food on your table to take a chance on something new with no safety net. But it doesn't have to be all or nothing. Save money, do your side hustle, gain experience, and devise your exit strategy.

Spend your time actually doing the thing that really lights you up. You don't have to do it on a stage to make it count—you can take baby steps to get there. Don't get stuck in an all-or-nothing mentality that dictates that you either chase your dreams or shackle yourself to security and give up hope for your future. That's crazy talk. Why can't you do both?

Success May Take Time, and That's OK

I coach a lot of new coaches who are still in their financially successful day jobs. I tell them do not quit your day job and leap into coaching. My wise mentor, executive coach Michele Woodward, told me that it usually takes at least three years to build a coaching business to the point where you are cash positive. At the time she told me this I was about eighteen months in and banging my head against a wall because I thought I was doing something wrong. I wasn't making enough money to take my coaching practice from a hobby to an actual financially solvent business. Learning this actually made me feel better and helped me to plod on and build the business I have today, and I wish more people were honest about the realities of starting a business. I'm sure there are lots of exceptions to the "at least three years rule," but for the most part it takes that long to gain traction.

If your dream job involves working for someone else and it comes with a paycheck, good for you! There's no shame in that. I love watching clients transition to jobs in unrelated fields, especially when they previously thought it wasn't possible. In our lifetime, we may cycle through several careers, and that's a good thing. We don't have to white-knuckle it through a job we hate for our entire careers anymore; it's okay to have a little of this and a little of that.

Dude, Get a Hobby

Most importantly, be sure to make time to do things you love, even if all they ever turn out to be is a hobby. Taking time to feed your soul in this way will bring you joy in ways that will sustain you even if you don't love your current position. Hobbies make us interesting and unique and are a wonderful creative outlet. And you never know where they will take you or who you might meet in the process!

If you love to sing, but you're a receptionist, sing anywhere you can—church, karaoke night, the car, the shower, or community theater. If you love to paint, PAINT for crying out loud! Get a canvas and go crazy. Stop waiting for an engraved invitation from the Universe that says, "You are hereby granted permission to do that thing you love to do right now." That day will never come. You need to make it a priority and ruthlessly cut out distractions to make it happen.

The antidote to turning tricks is living in integrity. Integrity is doing what you say you're going to do when you say you're going to do it. It's what you do when no one else is looking. Integrity is staying true to who you are and acting accordingly. When we are in integrity with ourselves, we are incorruptible—unable to act in ways that are incongruent with what we believe in. When we are in integrity, we do not do one thing and say another. We've gotta walk our talk, or as Martha Beck says, "live it to give it."

Being a life coach keeps me honest by doing regular integrity checks. I would feel like a lowlife creep if I gave my clients advice that I didn't actually follow myself. I regularly make sure that I'm doing my best to remain trustworthy!

Walk Your Talk

To write this book, I bitched and kvetched for eighteen months about how I *reallllly* wanted to write a book on MOJO and how I didn't have enough time to write it, and how I needed to make time to do it (but never actually did).

The turning point came when I committed to stop whining and start writing. First, I put writing this book on the top of my priority list, literally. Second, I cut out all the distractions I could to make the writing time happen. This meant saying no to teaching classes I enjoy teaching with a dear friend who I love. It meant not feeding my creative entrepreneurial spirit by devising new offerings and ventures because I needed to funnel every ounce of creativity I had into completing this mission.

I didn't stop there. I tightened up my coaching practice by primarily coaching one-on-one clients and mentoring two coaching groups. I asked other facilitators to teach my monthly life coaching meetup group so that

I didn't have to create any new classes while I wrote.

All of this meant I had to get dead serious about making this book a reality. Telling myself I would write a book someday but not doing it felt like I was selling out. Like I was selling myself short with excuses—and it didn't feel good. Especially because I'm someone who makes a living helping people live their best life! I would be a hypocrite if I kept this book inside of me, too afraid to prioritize the process and let it out for everyone to see.

Watch for the Universe to Conspire on Your Behalf!

When the Universe saw that I was indeed serious about making this happen, it actually did conspire to help me accomplish my goal, in ways I didn't expect, or necessarily like. Two classes I had already committed to teach before I prioritized writing the book didn't have enough enrollees, so I had to cancel them. A couple of clients who weren't my ideal people dropped off. I'll admit it; I got spooked.

But then another client, one of my ideal clients, asked me if I wanted help writing. She's a writer herself with an interest in coaching and had always wanted to try out what it would be like to be a writing coach. I nearly wept with relief to have someone in my corner so that I didn't feel so alone in the process.

Then I met a woman who had written a great book on finances, and while talking I mentioned that I had begun my own book. She went out of her way to give me her editor and book designer's information to help me! Again, I felt so grateful, and I took it as a nod from the Universe that I am on the right track and that I am guided and loved through this journey.

In other words, make what you want a priority and the Universe will carve out a path!

Keeping your integrity with *yourself* is one of the most important things you can do. Make sure that you aren't holding yourself back and selling yourself out. Make promises to yourself and keep them the way you would keep a promise to someone you care about. Don't let yourself down by making excuses for why you can't accomplish your goal. Make a plan and stick to it. Get an accountability partner to help you!

MOJO in Motion...

What is something you've wanted to accomplish but have been putting off and making excuses as to why?

_____

Who do you know that would help you stay accountable to yourself to accomplish your goal?

_____

Do you need to prioritize your life differently to get this done? If so, what needs to fall off the list to put this at the top?

_____

Focus on how you will feel when you have accomplished your goal—write the feeling you will have here:

_____

Create a mantra to help you stay on task, something that gets you excited about continuing: ex. "I am helping people find their MOJO with this book!"

_____

Put a deadline on that sucker. Most people work best with some fire under their ass. Backward plan to come up with an estimate of how long you need to complete your goal and get to it!

My goal will be complete by....

Chapter 14:
MOJO Killer #7
Turtle Shell Syndrome

"You mustn't be afraid to sparkle a little brighter, darling."
~ Kirsten Kuehn

Oh to be shiny…but, what does that mean? Well, I think it is to stand out from the crowd, to be seen, to sparkle a bit more than the rest.

What does being shiny mean to you? Are you comfortable with that kind of attention? Does it feel awkward or exciting? What happens when all eyes are on you?

Do you feel that your friends and family support you when you're shiny, or do you feel that they really would like to knock you down a peg and keep you a little less shiny?

A Shell Is a Shield

A turtle's shell protects the little critter's soft self from damage. That's understandable and very helpful when it's protecting itself from the impending doom of big, sharp teeth. But, if the turtle always hid its head, arms, and legs, it would never go anywhere and never see anything. It would be hiding from life.

So many people live this way that it breaks my heart. They keep their turtle shell up as a shield *all the time*. Yes, this protects them from harm—but it also prevents them from feeling love, taking a risk, exploring possibilities and living out loud.

In some families, being seen is dangerous—it may set you up for abuse or unwanted attention. It may seem safer to remain invisible and not make waves than to be seen. In this case, we need to update our mental programming to a new operating system. We are no longer children without power, we are adults with choices and control over our lives. It is safe to come out of the shadows.

In essence, people living in turtle shells are stuck: never moving backward, but never moving forward either. Without any propulsion, life gets very, very dull and can move one to ask "Is this all there is?" If you find yourself asking this question, look deep within you and ask if you are afflicted with Turtle Shell Syndrome.

We all need to ask ourselves how we feel about being seen—really seen. Especially if we are being seen for something that is important to us. If the answer is that it makes you nervous or not completely comfortable, you can rest assured that you are holding yourself back or sabotaging yourself because you have a fear of being seen in all your glory. **It's impossible to grow and protect yourself at the same time.**

You're denying your MOJO.

"Don't let someone dim your light simply because it's shining in their eyes." ~ *unknown*

The antidote to turtle shell syndrome is to shine on!

My friend Cyndi (who took me to the Oprah conference!) is incredible with packaging. Yes, packaging. She makes incredible handmade tags to go on anything from a birthday present to the lemonade jar at a party. When I remark upon it, she tells me, "It's nothing. Any idiot with a computer program and a glue gun can do it." But lots of people have the same program and a glue gun and they never think to do it. Or if they do, it doesn't look like Cyndi's rendition. She makes the ordinary into something extraordinary, because detail is something she takes pride in executing with excellence. Cyndi doesn't have to go into a career as a packaging engineer. But knowing that she is amazing with spicing up the ordinary to make it beautiful—we've got ourselves a MOJO clue!

Most of us are taught to be humble, to not seek attention for our talents, to act like our sparkly parts are "no big deal." That way, no one can ever accuse us of having a big ego, being stuck up, or behaving like an attention whore. We all want to avoid being branded with the "who does she think she is/she ain't all that/ he thinks he is pretty special/a legend in his own mind" type of labels.

So instead, we fly low under the radar, secretly hoping someone will notice that we speak four languages fluently, play piano like a prodigy, sing like Adele, dance like Usher, host spectacular dinner parties for twenty with ease, nurture babies like a mama bear, or design websites like Van Gogh paints *The Starry Night*.

Shiny Is Good! Arrogant Is not.

Do not mistake being shiny for being arrogant. They are not one and the same. Arrogance claims superiority. Shininess means unmasking a quality, talent, or skill that is intrinsic to who you are. My favorite definition of shiny is "filled with light, as by sunshine." Dimming your brightness can be disingenuous and somewhat disrespectful to your creator and to yourself. We were born to shine!

Are You Hiding?

Did you ever see the old cartoon with the singing frog, Michigan J. Frog? Check it out on YouTube if you haven't. It's a really funny bit about this frog that sings and dances with a top hat and cane, but only in front of his owner. The frog refuses to sing or dance in front of anyone else, which thwarts the owner's dreams of making easy cash by putting his singing frog on stage. The moment his owner brings anyone to see him sing, Michigan goes back into his box and croaks like a regular old frog, complete with a vacant expression on his face. It drives the poor owner crazy that he's the only one who sees the frog come to life!

How are you like Michigan J. Frog? What cool talents do you selfishly hoard and not allow others to witness? Yes, I know that sounds harsh, but I think it's a great way to think about it. Imagine if inventors decided that their cool airplane/automobile/cell phone/television/computer/light bulb would just attract too much attention and make them seem obnoxious if they shared their new invention with the world.

Imagine if they doubted the usefulness of their invention and kept it hidden under their bed rather than putting it out to the masses. That would be a tragedy!

Bask in Your Success!

When you do something awesomely, and others remark upon it, by God, **bask in it!** It's a wonderful thing to be able to give a beautiful compliment, and an exquisite gift to be able to receive it well and really welcome it into your heart. If you don't take a compliment well, you may as well just tell the giver that they have horrible taste and no sense whatsoever. Seriously, learn to take a compliment, people! Allow yourself to squirm (on the inside) and just say "Thank you." The more you do it, the easier it gets.

Another reason many people have Turtle Shell Syndrome is that they are afraid being seen will lead to criticism or to no longer being a part of their crowd.

My husband Alex calls this "crabs in a bucket." If you've ever seen crabs in a bucket, you'll know what he means—as soon as one crab gets to the top of the bucket to escape, one of his nasty little frenemies reaches a claw up and drags his ass back down with the rest of them. You may see being successful as dangerous to your position with your clan. What will happen if your talents and abilities are seen and appreciated? Will you still fit in with your peeps? Are you afraid you'll be voted off the island for being too successful? Fear of success is Turtle Shell Syndrome to the max.

MOJO in Motion...

Here is your assignment, should you choose to accept it: Become a little bit public about a talent of yours. Show off just a tad. Allow the compliments to pour over you and marinate in them. Notice any discomfort you may encounter, and then let that discomfort roll off your back. When you are all done, realize that you survived the experience. You shared one of your gifts with another, and were recognized for it. Feel how good it is to be seen, and rejoice!

Chapter 15:
MOJO Killer #8
Darth Vader Heart

"And the day came when the risk to remain tight in a bud was more painful than the risk it took to blossom."

~ Anaïs Nin

I could just as easily have called this particular MOJO killer "lack of vulnerability" or "aloofness sucks." Acting like you don't care or have no emotion distances you from others and sucks your MOJO clean off your bones. It may seem safe at first, but the risk of not letting other people in is far more detrimental to your MOJO than you might think.

Remember Darth Vader from *Star Wars*? Darth Vader Heart refers to the unfortunate person who has had their heart scorched, and then proceeds to insulate themselves—whether under a strangely-shaped black face mask and helmet or under a façade of aloofness.

Before Anakin Skywalker became Darth Vader, he was an idealistic, passionate man in love with Princess

Amidala (Padmé). He was a devoted son to his mother back on Tatooine.

What changed him into a heartless, evil villain?

When he got word that the Tuscan Raiders had captured and killed his mama, Anakin went on a revenge-killing spree that included men, women, and children. He later sold his soul to the dark side to keep Padmé and their unborn twins from harm. Anakin allowed his hate to consume him and he subsequently lost everyone he loved.

More Yoda, Less Darth

A Darth Vader Heart is one that has been eviscerated by pain and fear of loss. And as Yoda says, "Fear leads to anger, anger leads to hate, and hate leads to suffering."

There is no MOJO where pain, fear, and hate are allowed to thrive. These sensations dampen MOJO like a sopping wet blanket. If you are miserable, suffice it to say that your MOJO is a goner.

Beware of harboring resentment—it grows like black mold and corrupts your capacity to love. Silently seething with unspoken anger will kill a relationship and damage your health. When resentment has grown it's like an alpine lake contaminated by uranium. It negatively colors your perspective and gives rise to cynicism, which we'll discuss in the next chapter.

How to Heal a Darth Vader Heart:

1. Acknowledge your emotional pain. Stop denying that it's there and recognize it for what it is.
2. Allow yourself to feel it in your body. **We've got to feel it to heal it.** Let yourself feel the uncomfortable sensations that your psychic pain is causing. It won't last forever, I promise! According to neuroscientist Dr. Jill Bolte Taylor it only takes the body ninety seconds to process an emotion, whether positive or painful. One of my clients dealt with the death of her son by knowing that her grief would come in ninety-second waves, and that there would be a respite after the pain where she could breathe again.
3. Consciously release your pain and thank it for getting your attention so you could deal with it. Discharge any negative energy associated with it. Picture all of your pain washing through you into the earth.
4. Be compassionate with yourself and know that no feelings are "bad"—they may not feel good, but they are providing you with valuable information.
5. Accept what is. "This shouldn't be happening" is one of the most painful thoughts we can

think. It causes us to resist reality and judge it as wrong—which leads to stuffing our pain in our minds and, consequentially, in our bodies. Those stuffed emotions cause pain, disease, and stress.

The antidote to Darth Vader Heart is vulnerability. "I'm sorry, what? Vulnerability? I'd rather pluck out my own eyes than be vulnerable." That's a popular refrain when I tell my clients that the way to joy and fulfillment is through the door of vulnerability.

Brené Brown is a PhD professor from the University of Houston who has made a career out of researching vulnerability and shame. Her TED Talk on vulnerability went wildly viral and has been seen by millions. I highly recommend familiarizing yourself with her work, especially if you know you've got a shield around your heart or if you are having a tough time feeling joy.

To summarize, Brown contends that we cannot selectively numb painful emotions. Since we can't numb ourselves from pain without simultaneously and inadvertently numbing ourselves to joy, when we try too hard to guard against pain we can become numb to our lives—leading to a detached and unenthusiastic existence. True happiness comes from living "wholeheartedly," which by definition means we cannot just cleave off the parts that hurt and only get the good stuff. It doesn't work like that.

When Vulnerability Is Denied, Joy Becomes Foreboding

We as humans are meant to feel a full gamut of emotions, but somewhere along the way many of us have not only tried to protect ourselves from pain but have also walled ourselves off from feeling joy—because as Brené says, "when vulnerability is denied, joy becomes foreboding." We are terrified of joy because we are afraid it won't last, that the other shoe is bound to drop.

Obviously, this is no way to live. Living wholeheartedly is the way we heal a broken heart. Having trust in yourself that you can handle whatever comes your way is how you allow yourself to feel again. When we have trust in ourselves and our ability to be resourceful and resilient, we don't have to worry as much about being able to trust others—we know we are going to be okay *no matter what* because we know that we can trust ourselves.

Cultivate Vulnerability

No external threat can shake the foundation of your own personal power. We cannot go about the business of living with gusto if we are protecting ourselves from possible pain and suffering at the same time.

We must embrace authenticity to cultivate vulnerability. Authenticity is the daily practice of letting go of who we think we're supposed to be and embracing who we are.

MOJO in Motion...

Right now, write down three things you are a little afraid to be vulnerable about:

1)_____

2)_____

3)_____

Make a list of people within your circle of trust—people who have *earned the right* to hear your story. In other words, people you can trust to not use this information against you in the future, because they've kept their promises to you in the past:

1)_____

2)_____

3)_____

Practice being vulnerable with someone (or everyone) on this list. Tell them something you're nervous to talk about. Let your guard down a little. When you are able to share something vulnerable about yourself, you open the door for the other person to do the same. Start with something small—pick the least scary leap you can imagine to attempt first. You and your MOJO will feel the boost!

Chapter 16:

MOJO Killer #9
Haters Gonna Hate
(Cynicism Blows)

"Cynicism is not wisdom. Cynicism masquerades as wisdom, but cynicism is a self-imposed blindness. You put the blinders on yourself to protect yourself from a world that you think might hurt you or disappoint you. Be a fool. Believe things will be good.
Better to be hurt."
~ Steven Colbert

Let's face it—bitterness isn't sexy. Suspicion, believing the worst in everyone, and distrust stem directly from Darth Vader Heart, and we all know what happened to him. Not exactly a love magnet, is he?

Negativity is a repellent and a definite MOJO slayer. We all want to be around people who lift us up, make us feel special, and help us see the best in ourselves and the rest of the world. While a cynical comment now and then can be mildly amusing, a steady diet of it is corrosive and most detrimental to your MOJO.

The Call Is Coming from Inside the House!

Cynicism is an outward attack to thwart off feelings of sweetness and light, so as to protect a sad, needy little self from judgment and shame. It is a shield that prevents an attacker from sneaking in. The problem is that the call is coming from inside the house! It's like trying to mask the stench of a turd on your carpet by sprinkling baby powder over it. You have to remove the turd! No amount of artificial freshener can camouflage that shit.

Instead of allowing your heart to remain cynical, put a microscope up to that bad boy and see what's causing the damage. Is it nasty off-handed comments from family, friends, or coworkers you are supposed to feel safe with? Is it the gradual withering away of dreams you can no longer envision coming true? Perhaps it's anger you've turned inward upon yourself that has facilitated the decay of the most pure and unspoiled aspects of you.

The antidote to cynicism is hope and faith. The loss of hope that things can ever get better is a hotbed for the growth of cynicism, especially when it's cloaked in "realistic" words like "maturity," "reality," or "worldliness." When you give up believing that you can get what you want and start expecting that life will screw you over instead, you are putting a fork in your MOJO.

Don't let this be you! Begin a relentless examination of your underlying angry feelings and try to detect the thought patterns around them. Do you notice that you feel more cynical after a big disappointment? We often become cynical to distance ourselves from the pain of losing faith that things will get better because hope feels unattainable and foolish.

Keep Hope Alive!

We can convince ourselves that "the devil you know is better than the devil you don't." Sometimes we feel safer with the certainty that the world is a clusterfuck than with the hope that we can turn around the downward slide of global warming, wars across the globe, and hatred masked as righteousness. It may feel easier to act cynically after becoming overwhelmed with problems that we cannot find an answer to than to allow ourselves to dream of a better world.

Bringing cynicism from a global level to a personal level, a great example is how many people can become really negative about the prospects of finding love. I worked with one woman I'll call Beth. She'd been married twice before and was in a long-term relationship with a man who was emotionally abusive and manipulative. He criticized her endlessly, which wreaked havoc on her self-esteem. This beautiful, educated, fun-loving, and very accomplished woman felt so bad about herself that she allowed a man to treat her like garbage because she believed she was fundamentally flawed in some way. Beth even blamed herself—feeling like she must be sending out a beacon for men who would use and abuse her. Whenever she spoke about men, she became very cynical and came across as angry, hard, walled-off, and generally very prickly. What kind of message do you think that was sending to good men who might have been interested in her?

When in Misery, Change Your Thinking

We worked together for months to question her beliefs about men. I asked her to look for examples of good men doing good things. We made lists of relationships she knew of that seemed happy and respectful. At first she had tremendous trouble remembering any examples at all of relationships that were even slightly positive. Her cynical mind had glommed onto all the bad examples as proof that men were nasty takers with bad intentions.

I reassured Beth that she wasn't bad or crazy for having these associations around men—it was just her brain trying to protect her from pain and suffering. I asked her to thank the part of her brain that was sending out "Danger! Danger!" signals to her, and I prescribed large doses of self-compassion. Her fear-based reptile brain was just doing its job—trying to protect her from harm.

The change in Beth's thinking came when she was able to see that she'd linked men with pain. She made a concerted effort to turn those hurtful thoughts around. She began to meditate daily, listen to positive podcasts, go to gatherings with new upbeat people, and look for examples of great men doing noble things. We made a list of the qualities she wanted in a man and in her next relationship. Over the course of several months I could see a physical change in Beth. Her eyes sparkled and her body language softened. She smiled more and laughed easier. Her sense of humor even shifted from one of dark sarcasm to a lighter, happier tone. When she talked of others, she sounded much more compassionate and less judgmental. I watched this bitter woman blossom into an open, beautiful person filled with hope and optimism about the future.

Lo and behold, before long Beth met a man who had every characteristic she'd written about. At the time I met Beth, she didn't believe it was possible for her to find a man who was kind, loving, honest, and supportive, let alone tall, dark, and handsome—her qualifiers for a man were teeth and hair! It seemed too far-fetched that a man could share her hobbies, or be employed *and* successful. I haven't seen Beth in a while—because she's so damned happy she doesn't need me any more. (That's always my goal—to work myself out of a job!) Beth's transformation is one of the most amazing things I've witnessed and I am honored to have been a part of it.

MOJO in Motion...

Get quiet for a minute. Close your eyes and ask yourself where you've become cynical. You'll know it if there's an area of your life where you've lost hope that things will ever be any different. Maybe it's your finances? Your job? Your weight? Your health? Perhaps you're like Beth once was and believe that you'll never find real love. Let me tell you right now, you've got to change your thinking to recapture your MOJO. If you believe things will remain shitty and unfulfilling into perpetuity, you are creating a self-fulfilling prophecy that is keeping you down and crippling you with tunnel vision.

Begin to notice one positive thing about the area of your life you are feeling hopeless about. Notice a pain-free afternoon if you've got arthritis, or a lunch where you've chosen a salad instead of a cheeseburger. Put your attention on the positives in your life and allow yourself to have faith that you can be happier, healthier, or more prosperous. Your logical brain needs proof that a positive possibility exists, so write it down when you note any progress at all. Revisit this list often and allow your hope to catalyze change. Like we say about Santa Claus, if you believe you will receive.

Chapter 17:
MOJO Killer #10
Slothiness
(a.k.a. Lack of Urgency)

"Stuff your eyes with wonder," he said, "live as if you'd drop dead in ten seconds. See the world. It's more fantastic than any dream made or paid for in factories. Ask no guarantees, ask for no security, there never was such an animal. And if there were, it would be related to the great sloth which hangs upside down in a tree all day every day, sleeping its life away. To hell with that," he said, "shake the tree and knock the great sloth down on his ass."

~ Ray Bradbury

Ever known anyone who says they'll get around to really living their life *someday*—like when they retire, win the lottery, or get married? How about when their kids fly the coop, or when they finally ditch that shitty job? Yeah, me too. That attitude is kryptonite to a life coach. I want to shake people and say, "Show me *someday* on your calendar. I need to see it!" Your life is TODAY and it is a GIFT, and forgive me for being morbid, but it can be taken at any moment.

My mom died of breast cancer when she was forty-five years old. Her death shook me to my core and I promised myself I would live my life with urgency—never waiting for someday to roll around and make my dreams come true. I don't trust "someday." It's not real. It's out in the future and there is no power there; the only power is in this moment.

Watching my mom die young changed my outlook on life. I realized that life is indeed short and that we need to be shaken out of the complacency that raises our tolerance for bullshit.

Bullshit Loves Complacency

Living in a loveless marriage is bullshit. Being chained to a desk in a job you don't like for a corporation that doesn't care about you is bullshit. Putting up with bad behavior from family or friends is bullshit. Prioritizing money and prestige over people is bullshit. Waiting to feel better about anything is total bullshit.

How does this happen to us? None of us go into adulthood planning to put up with tons and tons of bullshit. And yet, so many of us do. Bullshit invades our lives like a thief in the night, and it steals our MOJO right out from under us. Tiny bit by tiny bit, our threshold for crap keeps getting a little bit higher until one day we don't recognize our lives or how we got there.

Bullshit Is a Thief

We put up with bullshit because we think it's temporary. Do not allow temporary to become permanent! Regaining a sense of urgency will lower your threshold for bullshit. You will soon realize you have a zero tolerance policy for BS and that you have reignited a fire under your ass to live your life the way you want to live it.

As rapper Young MC famously said, **"Don't just stand there, bust a move!" This is the antidote to slothiness.** Take inspired action and kick your own ass all the way to the finish line. Don't wait for the perfect time—you'll never find it. Don't wait for things to be perfect—they never will be. Done is better than perfect.

Procrastination is a big fat stalling technique we use when we don't think what we're doing is going to be good enough. Drop perfectionism like a bad habit—because it is. Excellence is a great target, but perfectionism shuts us down.

If you had one year to live, what would you do? You'd stop wasting time on bullshit, that's what you'd do. All of a sudden, your priorities would become crystal clear because you would be acutely aware of your mortality. Limited time requires action and demands that you drop perfectionism. Do a great job, but give yourself a deadline.

MOJO in Motion...

If you knew you only had one year to live....

- Would you stay in your romantic relationship?

  _____

- Would you keep your job?

  _____

- Would you spend your precious time with the friends and family you spend time with now?

  _____

- Would you spend your time the same way?

  _____

- What travel plans have you been putting off?

  _____

- What experiences would you pursue that you've been waiting for "someday" to do?

  _____

- What time-suckers and obligations would you ditch with your newfound awareness of the preciousness of time?

  _____

- What crap would you stop caring about because it's a waste of time and energy?

  _____

- What chances would you take knowing that it's now or never?

  _____

Reevaluate the way you spend your time and why you are holding yourself back from doing things that are important to you. You are never going to get this time back. Stop finishing books that suck. Stop watching inane TV shows and uninspired movies. Stop doing crap you don't care about because it might look good on your resume.

Stop it. Knock that shit off. MOJO is coupled with passion, not obligation. I'm writing you a permission slip right now to quit something that is not life or death but more like checking a box and that drains your life force.

You have a choice. Bust a move.

"Twenty years from now you will be more disappointed by the things that you didn't do than by the ones you did do. So throw off the bowlines. Sail away from the safe harbor. Catch the trade winds in your sails. Explore. Dream. Discover." ~ *Mark Twain*

Chapter 18:
MOJO Killer #11
All Work and No Play

"Beware the barrenness of a busy life."

~ Socrates

"It's not enough to be busy; so are the ants.
The question is: what are we busy about?"

~ Henry David Thoreau

"All work and no play doesn't just make Jill and Jack dull, it kills the
potential of discovery, mastery, and openness to change and flexibility,
and hinders innovation and invention."

~ Joline Godfrey

How do you feel when you've been working *wayyyy* too hard? Can you remember the last time you weren't focusing seriously on your extremely long and never-ending to-do list? Maybe it's been a very long time since you've laughed so hard that your belly ached and your cheeks hurt.

But MOJO can't seep in when there is no playfulness. MOJO likes to be welcomed in with ease, giggles, dancing, and general shenanigans. It cannot jump the hurdle of a furrowed brow.

Don't Let Busy Get in the Way of Play!

We've glorified the business of busy-ness in our culture to the point of being ridiculous and downright dangerous. It has become standard to answer "crazy busy!" when someone asks how we are. And it feels like we've left our right arm at home if we go somewhere without our phones! Go to any restaurant and you will see people sitting across from each other on their phones rather than talking to the person in front of them.

Think about it: whatever we pay attention to is our priority. We all say that family comes first, but is that really the case if we're always worried about and distracted by work? Checking our emails, texting our clients or boss, or working on our computers late into the night and on the weekend is not sending the message to our loved ones that they come first.

Busy shouldn't be how we describe our lives. *Busy doing what?* That's the question. Busy is not necessarily productive—it can be just running from one activity to another without any sense of purpose or feeling.

Pastor Rob Bell says, "Busy is a drug that a lot of

people are addicted to." We take drugs to numb pain and sometimes to create an altered state of consciousness. So if you're using "busy" as a drug, it implies there is something awry with your current reality that you need a constant distraction from. If your priority is making sure you are busy, I can promise you that you are running from something. There is something dashing through your brain on a consistent basis that is making you so uncomfortable that you'd rather have a flurry of constant (and not necessarily meaningful) activity rather than a moment of peace.

Busy-ness Does Not Equal Worthiness

Being busy doesn't equate to being worthy—but that's a mistake many people make. Hustling for our sense of worthiness has become a first-world expectation. Trying too hard is killing our MOJO, y'all. It's a crying shame that we are chasing self-worth through *doing doing doing*, when all we have to do is start *being being being*. There's a difference, you know.

When you're too busy, MOJO can't find an opening. It can't work its magic when you are eating your dinner in your car while driving to your kid's baseball practice while talking on the phone while listening to a podcast. It looks crazy written down, right? But we've all done it!

MOJO comes out of hiding when there's an opportunity, when you allow yourself to come out of the fight or flight response and unwind a little.

The antidote to all work (or busy-ness) is play.
Putting in a lot of effort feels tense and heavy. Playing feels light and easy—and that's when MOJO comes for a visit. When you don't take yourself and your life so seriously, your MOJO can come out and play.

By no means am I saying lie around and pick your nose all day long. What I'm saying is to make time to rejuvenate yourself often with some sort of relaxation or play. Time you spend on that is more productive than you can even imagine. Research shows that play improves brain function, prevents memory loss, alleviates stress, boosts immunities to illness, and fosters creativity—in other words, it restores you.

Play is a state of mind, not necessarily a concrete activity. While performing everyday tasks, find ways to incorporate more play. Break into song and dance regularly. Listen to more music. Keep a little bouncy ball in your pocket and whip it out periodically during your day. Blow bubbles. Play fetch with your dog. I implore you—don't act your age. Being an adult is highly overrated. Take behaving like a child to a whole new level. Playfulness is fun, sexy, and crazy good for MOJO-making.

MOJO in Motion...

Schedule a play date for yourself. Notice how good it feels to wander aimlessly without a specific goal in mind. Some seriously good ideas and some good feeling MOJO can come about from this place!

If it has been so long since you had a play date that you can't even remember how, here are some ideas:

- Make play dough sculptures
- Take a walk
- Get a massage
- Go to the park
- Paint a picture
- Sing at a karaoke bar
- Go bowling
- Play with your dog
- Ride your bike
- Go to a comedy club
- Turn the music up and dance in your living room
- Be silly

If you'd like more scientific proof that play is therapeutic and food for productivity, take a few minutes to watch psychiatrist Stuart Brown's TED Talk called "Play is more than just fun."

(http://www.ted.com/talks/stuart_brown_says_play_is_
more_than_fun_it_s_vital?language=en)

Play Facilitates Success!

Here's a real-life example of how a bit of play can make a big difference. Tess, a very dignified and highly competent woman, worked in sales for a large corporation. She had a disciplined and controlled demeanor that some people found detached and aloof, which really wasn't helping her sales much. Tess hired me to help her find her work MOJO—which meant to rediscover her love for her work and increase her sales numbers.

I noticed that when she spoke of her dog her eyes lit up, her face softened, and she smiled brightly. Her energy changed immediately—she became more approachable, more joyful, and frankly, more fun. I asked her to spend more time playing with her dog and less time strategizing for her next sales call. I also asked her to watch videos of her dog being adorable before she went into a meeting with a potential client.

Tess looked at me as if I'd asked her to quit her job and become a magic pixie. I explained to her that she was far more relatable as a person when she loosened up and had more fun. I suggested she connect with her prospects on a heart level as well as on a mental level. She already had everything else going for her—high integrity, deep knowledge base, great reputation, and thorough follow-through skills. The only piece that was missing was the MOJO.

Despite her misgivings she did what I suggested, and

the results were astounding—within a year, her sales numbers went from the middle of the pack to number one in the nation. No lie. Not from working harder, but from allowing herself to play and by conveying the more jovial part of her nature. Remember, we want to work with people we like, so when we make ourselves more approachable and fun, people will gravitate toward us like kids chase the ice cream man!

Chapter 19:
MOJO Killer #12
Stage Fright

"Nervousness is just excitement in need of an attitude adjustment."
~ Unknown

Imagine that you've been looking forward to seeing your favorite band in concert for months, and when the lights go down and the music starts, you can tell the lead singer is nervous. Maybe he isn't really looking at the crowd, or he's fidgety and keeps messing around with his earpiece. Your guy looks really uncomfortable, shifty, and uncertain. You can smell his fear a mile away. A scared rock star has no MOJO.

What would you think? How do you think the energy in the arena would respond?

We've all had performance anxiety. All of us want to have grace under pressure and knock it out of the park when our time to shine is upon us. The stress of trying to be perfect and avoid criticism creates performance anxiety.

Use Your Fear as Fuel

What if you could harness this fear and use it as fuel to energize you, rather than as an obstacle that disables you? Ever notice that sometimes it's hard to tell if you are nervous or excited? They feel very similar, don't they? Butterflies in the stomach, buzzy feeling in your body, jittery hands and feet.

Nervousness is very different from true fear. Real fear is the impetus for your body's fight-or-flight response. It can look like running from a burning building, curling up in a ball to survive the fallout of a blast, or fighting for your life in the face of an attacker. It's a physiological response to survive any dangerous situation that comes your way.

Nervousness is when your head gets in the picture. When you start thinking the worst and cluttering your brain with "what if" scenarios, you've gone past fear and straight to anxiety.

Anticipation feels like envisioning the future in an excited way. If you are anticipating what may come of a conversation, an audition, an interview or a vacation, you are in your head thinking about all of the great possibilities that may await you when the thing you are looking forward to comes to pass.

The antidote to performance anxiety is to feel the adrenaline rush of excitement in your body and move with a purpose. Rather than letting this anxiety sidetrack you, channel it into excitement. Allow the energy pumping through your system to push you into taking a step toward what you want. Get out of your head where expectations hover and fully inhabit your body to take inspired action. Stop trying to control the outcome and allow yourself to get lost in the movement you are creating. Go with your gut and let yourself get carried away!

If you are giving a presentation at work, but you seem nervous and unsure—you've bludgeoned your MOJO. But, if you can remember how you felt after the last time you gave a talk *and* you *killed* it, you're putting yourself into the realm of excitement rather than anxiety.

Get out of Your Head and into Your Theme Song...

Remember when we were teenagers and we had a mix tape for every occasion? (Yes, I realize I am dating myself with that statement, but I am a child of the '80s, dammit!) My husband teases me mercilessly about the seventeen ancient cassette tapes labeled "Keisha's Funky Songs" that I refuse to dispose of.

My girlfriends and I would play a tape while we were getting ready to go out, and in the car on the way. There were mix tapes for every occasion—"Beach Music," "Dance Mix," "Car Tunes," and "Girls Just Wanna Have Fun!" Just broke up with a boyfriend? Just play Alanis Morissette's "You Oughta Know" really loud a few thousand times until your neighbors beg you to take him back.

Why did we go to all of that effort? Because music puts us in a mood. *Mood music*, right? Now we have playlists—but sometimes we only use those for working out. (Maybe sometimes for cleaning—I personally enjoy mopping to Journey. Well, not exactly *enjoy*, but it makes the task more tolerable!) I realized how much I missed music when I started listening to it again while I was getting ready in the morning. Apps like Pandora are a beautiful thing. For the last several years I have been rockin' out while drying my hair and brushing my teeth. I see the effect it has on my mood, and I wonder how I ever forgot to use this amazing Prozac-like tool.

As soon as I rediscovered this, I decided that I needed a theme song. You know, like Rocky...or Ally McBeal. I figured if I came up with my own song that motivated me I could conquer the world! So every few months I decide on a new theme song. For a while it was Taylor Swift's "Shake It Off," then it was "Uptown Funk" by Mark Ronson and Bruno Mars. I've got theme songs from Amy Winehouse, The Commodores, The Black Eyed Peas, The Beatles, and more. Now I play these songs whenever I want to get into my zone, and it works—every single time.

Since it's worked so well for me, I ask my clients to find a theme song for themselves. Not only do they feel triumphant when they find their song, but they thoroughly enjoy the process of finding it. Looking for your theme song brings you back to your youth when you found comfort and understanding in the lyrics of your favorite artists. It immerses you in a long-forgotten world where you are out of your head and following your feel-good! It's like going on a treasure hunt through your past, allowing the music to remind you of feeling carefree, happy, creative, sexy, or powerful. Once you find your theme song, hang onto it as long as it feels good. Feel free to change it when you want, or find a theme song for any emotion you want to evoke.

MOJO in Motion...

Here's how to find your theme song...

1) Listen to music
2) See what energizes you
3) Wait to see which song gets stuck in your head
4) Analyze how you feel when you hear it
5) Repeat until satisfied

Finally, something that makes us feel good that is healthy, cheap, and easy! Let me know what you come up with. Now rock on with your bad self!

My MOJO Idol: Beyonce' Inspired Coaching Tools

You may remember that Beyoncé is one of my MOJO idols. When I can channel my inner Beyoncé (or Sasha Fierce!) some epic shit can get done.

A while ago, I was coaching a client on her relationship with a man who wasn't treating her with the respect she deserved.

My client wanted more of a commitment, but he continually failed to show up for her at crucial moments when she needed him.

As I was listening to her, the Beyoncé song "Irreplaceable" popped into my head. You know the one: *"To the left, to the left—everything you own in a box to the left."*

(Being an intuitive coach, this kind of thing happens to me all the time and I share these intuitive blips with certain clients if I think they might be helpful.)

A few minutes later, my client told me of her partner's jealousy about a man who had just asked her out...and immediately a new Beyoncé song started playing... *"Don't be mad once you see that he want it, if you liked it then you shoulda put a ring on it."*

Of course, because it's me—and I have a sass mouth—I sang these little hooks to her. She burst out laughing, realizing that I still saw her as the spunky woman that she had forgotten herself to be.

You knew that Beyoncé is known for songs about female empowerment—but who knew that she's the mastermind behind some awesome coaching tools on a virtual cornucopia of topics?

Refer to the following songs by Queen Bey...

On independence—"Independent Woman"

On perseverance—"Survivor"

On body confidence —"Bootylicious"

On loyalty—"Irreplaceable"

On commitment—"Single Ladies

(Put a Ring on It)"

Use these Beyoncé coaching tools to recover your sass. Make sure you have a fan blowing on you at all times, and don't forget to wear your body suit and stiletto heels.

Chapter 20:
MOJO Killer #13
Energy Vampires

"We humans have always sought to increase our personal energy in the only manner we have known, by seeking to psychologically steal it from the others--an unconscious competition that underlies all human conflict in the world."

~ James Redfield, "The Celestine Prophesy"

In the past decade, it seems that all things "vampire" have become cool—the wildly successful *Twilight* series, *True Blood*, etc. However, one kind of vampire is definitely an exception: the energy vampire. Dr. Judith Orloff defines energy vampires as "people who suck the serenity and optimism right out of you." No matter what you call them, you know one when you see one, or rather, when you *feel* one.

Unfortunately, once we fall into their clutches we may not be able to pry ourselves out of their desperate grasp until significant damage is already done. Depending on the skill of the vampire at hand and how long you've been around them, once they start to drain you it could be hours, days, or even weeks or months before you start to feel like yourself again. These soul suckers are a stake through the heart of your MOJO.

How to Know if Your MOJO Is Being Siphoned

Here are the signs you are in the clutches of an emotional vampire:

- You get the urge to bolt, but for some reason feel like you are standing in quicksand.
- You are afraid to seem impolite, and keep trying to think of possible ways to get out of the conversation.
- You feel you are supposed to care about or feel sorry for the person speaking, but you don't.
- You may be asking yourself, "Why is this person telling me this?"
- Your gut is screaming "DANGER," but you remain strangely passive and unsure of yourself.
- You feel sleepy, very sleepy.
- You may feel attacked or "slimed."
- You may get the urge to drink a cocktail or eat some comfort food.

I always tell my clients to pay attention to how they feel when they leave a person, group, or environment. If you leave an interaction feeling any of the above-mentioned ways, ask yourself what about it caused you to feel icky. If you see a pattern where you usually feel yucky after you see someone, it's time for a relationship evaluation.

The vampire brings you in with a tentacle, attaches with a vice-like grip, and holds on until you are sucked under. They do it by hooking you with drama, stirring up your emotions, or pushing your buttons. I was recently co-facilitating a group when a woman decided it was time to tell her life story as the group was gathering their things to leave.

She launched into a drama-filled rant in which she carefully left breadcrumbs of worry for her safety, leading us to ask her if she needed a restraining order. It was only a few minutes into her story before I realized this woman was an energy vampire. She continued to talk ad nauseam and undeterred, even after participants began leaving the meeting! It was only after several facilitators stood up and pushed in our chairs that she stopped talking. I left feeling like I'd been held hostage, slimed, and depleted. The next morning I still felt crappy, and then I remembered what this vampire had told us her profession was. She's a phlebotomist—she takes people's blood for a living. Honest to God, true story! The metaphor of the situation was beyond belief.

You are in danger of attracting an energy vampire if:

You are a people pleaser, a "nice" person, hate being rude, need work on your self esteem, have depression, or routinely play the role of victim.

We tend to attract vampires who mirror unresolved issues in ourselves. Once we can find the pattern, we can work on healing it so that we can develop a super-shield against it, rather than a funnel for attracting it.

Save the Drama for Yo Mama

Years ago, a hugely popular book by James Redfield called *The Celestine Prophecy* outlined four "control dramas" that are ways people try to draw energy from one another.

- **Intimidators** steal energy by bullying others into submission.
- **Interrogators** steal power by judging and questioning.
- **Aloof people** control by pulling attention and energy toward them by withdrawing.
- **Victims** (aka **"Poor me!"**) control by making others feel guilty and responsible for their happiness.

Notice which control dramas are used by you and against you. Manipulating for power and control is a shadow side of human behavior. It stems from insecurity and the belief that we must be in control of others in order to feel whole and secure.

The antidote for emotional vampires is learning to create healthy boundaries.

Pick a Boundary, Any Boundary

For a long time, I thought the word "boundary" meant a border crossing in a foreign land, where a man holding a gun shouts menacingly in a language I don't understand about crimes I can't remember perpetrating.

So when my therapist suggested that I "create some healthy boundaries" in some troublesome relationships in my life, I felt strangely guilty, as if putting any distance or barrier at all between myself and a friend or family member was heresy, and that I might be voted off the island for the audacity of the mere thought. I've since realized that being completely enmeshed with people I love makes it hard to live my own life, and makes it impossible to stay in my own business. Knowing when to get close and when to pull back is a dance worth learning.

> *"**Personal boundaries** are guidelines, rules or limits that a person creates to identify for him- or herself what are reasonable, safe and permissible ways for other people to behave around him or her and how he or she will respond when someone steps outside those limits. They are built out of a mix of beliefs, opinions, attitudes, past experiences and social learning."*
> ~ *Wikipedia*

If you're like me, you probably grew up in a family where you were taught to accept kisses from long-lost relatives, even those with strange smells and scratchy faces. "No thank you, creepy Great Aunt Bessie, I do not want to come sit on your lap," was not an appropriate response when an adult demanded your cooperation.

It's confusing to know when it's expected that you please someone else, and when to assert your independence. Unfortunately, we aren't taught that we can renegotiate our own zone of comfort when we grow up. I welcome you to turn my pain into your cautionary tale.

I Knew I Had "Boundary Issues" When....

I realized I needed to look into getting some of these boundary thingies when I was gagging on paint fumes at a disorganized "poor me" energy vampire's, errr...I mean, friend's house many years ago. I'll call her Debbie (as in Downer!). Being witness to the never-ending string of unfortunate events that was her life, I could barely control my urge to "fix" her—*because she had so much potential!!!* Debbie was on bed rest while waiting for the birth of her third child, so I took it upon myself to clean up her nest before the baby was born.

I was painting her baseboards with a fresh coat of eggshell white, after I had steam cleaned her carpet, scrubbed her chair cushions, and washed her walls with soap and water. She munched popcorn cheerfully in front of *Days of Our Lives*, casually moving her feet so that I could move her furniture.

This would all have been lovely of me to do if I felt the relationship was a two-way street and I was truly being helpful from a pure place in my heart. It would have been generous if we had a back-and-forth habit of doing things for one another. But…what was really happening was that Debbie's house was a perpetual hot mess and it made me uncomfortable (practically break out into hives, really) to be there. I don't think it actually bothered her much at all, and she was rather unappreciative of my efforts. I was always in the helper mode because it satisfied her need to be taken care of and my need to feel "good enough," and possibly even superior.

Sadly, I was putting my hard work into an imaginary investment account for our friendship, thinking that if I put in enough good deeds, I would be deserving of similar acts of service if my time of need ever came. The problem was that this friend never knew about the "investment account" I had opened—so how could she ever know it was time for her to put in a deposit rather than continuing to make withdrawals? I became resentful in the friendship because I was always busy doing for her, while she never volunteered to do anything for me.

If I had known then what I know now, I would have realized that this vampire was not equipped to give back any of the energy I directed her way. It was like hoping that a fish would climb a tree because I made it a really nice sandwich.

I didn't feel like I was enough, so I thought I needed to do things for people in order for them to like me and want to be my friend. Please learn from my ridiculous attempt to please. Volunteering to slave away for a bloodsucker does not make you a virtuous, indispensible friend; it makes you a resentful martyr. Martyr MOJO=NO MOJO. (Incidentally, Debbie's house went right back to being a tragic wreck a few weeks after my "makeover.")

How Do You Know if Your Boundaries Suck?

Do you feel overwhelmed, resentful, exasperated, or imposed upon?

You'll know you need to set stronger personal boundaries if you:

1. Have relationships that feel icky and you don't know how to get out.
2. Feel exhausted by other people's problems and think others need you to help them.
3. Find yourself worrying more about how someone else feels about you than how you feel about them.

On the other hand, do people ever describe you as intimidating, reserved, distant, or prickly?

You'll know if you need to loosen up your boundaries if you:

1. Can't remember the last time you asked someone else to have lunch, but you sure wish someone would ask you.
2. Find that people are formal with you, and seem hesitant to include you in the "what did you do this weekend?" banter.
3. Have trouble recollecting a time when you took a risk and divulged something personal about yourself.

OK, I Need Better Boundaries. Now What Do I Do?

1. Pay attention to how you feel when you are with a person or a group of people, or when immersed in an activity. Pay special attention to how you feel when you leave an interaction—look at your energy level. Do you feel deflated or off? Do you have a sudden urge to inhale a dozen cookies? Are you tired or drained? Being aware of how you feel around other people or in certain situations is the first step to knowing where you are losing personal power, and with whom.

2. Make a list of people and situations in which you notice that you feel like a diminished version of yourself. Start a list with the first five people or situations you can think of right now:

_____

_____

_____

_____

_____

3. Choose a person from the above list and ask yourself why you keep engaging with this person (or keep putting yourself in this situation). Have you been assertive and clear about what you do and don't like about the relationship? Are you able to vocalize your needs or are you afraid that having needs will jeopardize the relationship?
4. What do you find yourself regularly complaining about? That will be a clear indicator of where your boundaries could use some shoring up.
5. Remember a time when your boundaries were clearly violated. Can you put yourself back in time and feel into your body? How did it feel? Where did you feel it? Can you give it a name that

you'll remember so that when it happens again you can identify that feeling? If you get even a tinge of that feeling again, you'll know in present time that your boundaries are being crossed.

6. Learn appropriate language to stop boundary crossing in its tracks. Rehearse it so that you will have it handy when you need it, because boundary crossers are sneaky. They use surprise guerilla tactics just when you least suspect it! See the list below if you need a script.

7. Again, as Brené Brown says *"Choose discomfort over resentment."* Be courageous enough to endure some short-term uneasiness to help build your long-term MOJO.

"Choose discomfort over resentment" is my new mantra. I am trying to remain present when I get the first inkling that I feel like my boundaries are being invaded. I've learned that when I can voice my feelings in the moment, or at least very soon thereafter, I can keep myself from going to Crazytown, otherwise known as "self-doubt." Visualize what a life with less obligation, more authenticity, and expanded personal power would look like for you. Keep that vision firmly in your mind before you agree to something you don't really want to do.

Hand Over the Appropriate Boundary and Nobody Gets Hurt.

Over the years I've come to realize that boundaries do not come in one-size-fits-all. They can be customized to fit the person and whatever situation we find ourselves in.

Exhibit A:
I have a Swiss cheese boundary with Alex, my husband of twenty-four years. It's aged, thin, flexible, transparent, contains holes, and sometimes it stinks if I don't properly care for it. He loves me, protects me, is faithful to me—**and** a thoughtless or unkind word from him can send me reeling. To let all of his deliciousness in, I have to accept that there are security breaches in my queso.

Exhibit B:
People who have hurt me—badly, time and time again—get a Great Wall of China boundary. It's long, wide, deep, impenetrable, and stony silent. I have done all I can do with a person who receives the Great Wall treatment, and I realize that their very presence is toxic and completely unworkable. I've learned that this sort of protection is even doable when you love someone— because it is possible to love from a safe distance with no communication necessary. This allows room for people

who treat me with respect and love rather than disdain and derision. Dr. Robin Smith says, *"When you indulge someone in poor behavior, in ways in which disrespecting you and not honoring you is actually permitted and you accept it, that sends the wrong message—as if it is okay,"*

Exhibit C:

Most of the people I know fall somewhere in between the Great Wall and lacy cheese on the boundary continuum—like a lovely French door. I see those behind it in the most positive and beautiful light. There's a clean wood edge around the outside, framed, definitive and decorative. When the glass gets cloudy I clean it off with Windex, or truth, whatever works. I can unlock the door if I feel safe and welcoming to what's on the other side, or I can close it and maintain a secure perimeter while keeping my options open. The great thing about a French door is that it is equally attractive open or closed. I get to choose based on my mood and the circumstances whether I let people into my space, or respectfully keep them at an arm's length.

When people who fit into this boundary category ask me to do something, I take life coach Cheryl Richardson's advice and follow the guideline that *"If it's not an absolute 'yes,' then it's a 'no."* Meaning—when someone requests something from you, you will know if it is something you really want to do because you will feel no reluctance whatsoever. In fact, you may even feel flattered or excited by the request. Answering no is appropriate when the request feels sticky, icky, manipulative, or pressuring. If you feel you "should" want to do it, but you don't —you are shoulding on yourself. If you feel like it's something you are obligated or "supposed" to do, fulfilling the request may lead to resentment toward yourself and the person asking.

This is what Brené Brown means by choosing discomfort over resentment. It's uncomfortable to say no to someone, but it's better for the relationship in the long haul if you are brave enough to tolerate that emotion rather than becoming resentful.

As Dr. Susan Biali says *"Guard your life energy, it's the most important currency you have."*

HELP! I Need a Script!

Here are some examples of language you can use to assert a boundary...

"I feel uncomfortable discussing my weight with you. Let's talk about something else."

"It hurts my feelings to hear you say that."

"I'd love to come to your party, but I really need to spend some time with my family."

"I would be happy to give you some ideas of how to handle that situation, but this is actually how I make my living. Would you like to make an appointment?"

"I'm sorry I can't meet with you. My plate is very full right now."

"Your charity is a very worthy cause, but I have my own charities that I contribute to. Good luck!"

"Right now isn't really the time or place to have this discussion."

"I'm finding that it's crucial for me to have down time where I have nothing scheduled for the sake of my health and sanity!"

"I'm up to my eyeballs in volunteering for now. I'll let you know when my schedule opens up."

"I understand that you are having a tough time financially. I've found that loaning money can make relationships icky and I value ours too much for that to happen."

"Wow, you are both lovely people, but I am much too possessive over my husband to swing. Have fun!"

I love this one from my friend Marlice…"Oh, my husband and I have a policy—we don't help people move."

When confronted with a persistent boundary pusher, remember that NO IS A COMPLETE SENTENCE! If you can't bear to be that direct, cheerfully say "No thanks!" like my nephew does when asked if he'd like more revolting lima beans on his dinner plate.

It's been quite a long time since I painted anyone's baseboards, but sometimes I am still tempted to go over and do a little light dusting. At times like this, I try to remember that it is not my business to "fix" others when I have not been asked to do so, well-meaning as my intention may be, because I am depriving them of the chance to learn and grow on their own, not to mention the fact that it's probably annoying and misguided to assume that someone wants to be "fixed." (By the way, "fixed" and "coached" are not the same thing!)

If I apply the wrong boundary to the wrong person and end up too close to vampire territory, I high-tail it back behind the Great Wall, reassess, and lick my wounds. The French door allows me to flow back and forth seamlessly between getting to know others, and inviting them to see the real me. And only those within the circle of trust are getting invited over for some Swiss cheese fondue!

Francesca's MOJO Story

Sensuality savant, Dancing queen, MOJO all-star

Francesca was a beautiful, well-to-do, dark-eyed woman with a regal aura and the poise of a ballerina. She was married to a well-respected doctor and managed his large medical practice. Francesca came to see me at the lowest point in her life.

She told me that her husband of twenty years was threatening divorce and things were very tense at home. What Francesca didn't tell me during our first two sessions is that her very successful and worldly husband was beating the tar out of her. He was kicking and punching her during fits of rage and she had the broken bones and bruises to prove it.

For years, she had gone to parties, family get-togethers

and neighborhood dinners alone—which was sad since she was such a vivacious social butterfly. Her husband was always "working." Philandering was more like it.

The saddest part of the story was that Francesca still loved her husband and was tolerating his abuse because at least he was paying attention to her after years of neglect. She was willing to suffer the battering because she hoped it meant he still cared about her and that maybe they could resurrect the marriage that had died years before.

Then Francesca's husband filed for divorce, which sent her reeling. She was trying desperately to hang on to the life she thought she had, while largely denying that the abuse/neglect cycle had become as awful as it truly was.

Francesca left her fancy home in a gated community and moved into a small apartment with few of her personal belongings and none of her beloved pets. She was essentially locked out of her old life, and the overwhelming volume of court documents and disclosures paralyzed Francesca with fear. There was so much newness in her life, and none of it felt good to her. Suffice it to say that Francesca had the wind completely knocked out of her and she had no fight left.

After several months of working with her intensively, I noticed Francesca begin to slowly recover some of her self-esteem and her numbness started to defrost. A feisty woman with spunk and character started to emerge from the void and the work of rebuilding her life began. She laughed more easily, her sense of humor resurfaced, and over the course of a year I watched the trepidation she embodied melt away.

Underneath the demure, doctor's-wife facade was a fierce warrior with a shit-ton of MOJO! This woman was courageous, open, willing, and exceedingly brave. Once she honored rather than squelched the woman inside of her who had lots of opinions, quirks, zest, and chutzpah, she became an unstoppable MOJO machine!

Francesca plunged into spiritual seeking and developing her sense of self by going to seminars, classes, workshops, and other gatherings. She surrounded herself with a magnificent group of new friends to share her experiences with. Gone were the days of being a helper in the shadows—Francesca became a force of nature on her own.

Francesca is an extremely physical person. She loves working with her hands and enjoys taking on home improvement tasks. Francesca enjoys dancing and exercising and her love language is physical touch. So, she decided to become a massage therapist—which is a perfect combination of her desire to take care of others in a hands-on way. When Francesca finishes her courses and starts her business, she will be a very successful body worker because her work encapsulates all the best parts of her MOJO.

Since letting her sassy, confident, self-possessed self shine, Francesca is attracting potential mates like moths to a flame. Her other single friends are taking notes about how to do the same—and she is an excellent teacher. Her love of life and enjoyment of being a sensual woman ooze out of her being and are captivating to everyone in her presence. Francesca definitely got her MOJO back!

Chapter 21:
MOJO Killer #14
I've Got Friends in
Low Places

"Show me your friends, and I'll show you your future."
~ John Kuebler

It has been said that we become an amalgam of the five people we spend the most time with. If you've got the wrong cast of characters in your life, this can be a terrifying realization. Birds of a feather flock together.

So if you don't like how the five people you spend the majority of your time with make you feel, it's time to find a new posse!

Your Friends Are Mirrors

Hanging out with critical, negative people will not only dull your shine, but it also speaks volumes about what you will allow. The people around you are mirrors that show you how you feel about yourself. (The same is not only true about the character of your peeps, but also their financial situation. If you are hanging out with family or friends who are perpetually broke, good luck lifting your own finances out of the gutter.)

There are lots of reasons for this tendency to be at a similar level as those around us. Our environment is a reflection of our thoughts and actions. We are social creatures, so what we deem "normal" is directly correlated with what we see going on around us. If everyone we know is selling drugs, it becomes ordinary to us, and our own moral compass may shift to include that profession as a possibility. Conversely, if all of your peers are building homes for Habitat for Humanity on their spring break, it will seem quite normal for you to do so as well.

Just look around...rich people mingle with other wealthy people, famous people hobnob with other celebrities, religious people congregate with those of their own faith, pissed-off people associate with their angry cronies, and catty people chum around with other bitches.

Loving, positive people gravitate toward one another because like attracts like. If your cast of characters could use a tune up, you can go about fixing this two different ways. The first way is from the outside in.

The antidote to having friends in low places is to weed your garden of energy suckers and cultivate a team that nurtures and inspires your growth.

Change your cast of characters and start socializing with people who have what you want and who already are where you want to go. Think of recovering addicts; there is a reason that part of the recovery process for drug and alcohol addiction is to change your peer group. Recovering alcoholics need to stay out of bars and away from the party atmospheres where drinking is the social norm. Recovering drug addicts need to lose their drug dealer's phone number and stop hanging out with other people who are using.

Need Some New Peeps?

Begin spending time with people who are going in the direction you want to go. Are you a smoker trying to kick the habit? Stop going for coffee breaks with your other smoker friends. Take a walk instead; better yet, walk with a non-smoker and cultivate a new friendship. Trying to lose weight? Go to Weight Watchers with other folks with the same goal.

Meetup.com is a fantastic tool to find your people. There are zillions of different groups in your area that come together around a particular interest or affiliation. "Over-forty bisexual board game night" could be your next outing if you so desire! I host a women's life-coaching meetup and the greatest compliment someone can give me about the experience is *"This is where my people are! I feel at home."*

You want to grow? Follow your curiosity to learn

about things you've always wondered about. Go to places that will teach you new things. There are other people there who want the same things you do. Having a buddy to share the ride with makes it so much more rewarding.

Want to be more financially abundant? Ask people who have the money thing wired about how they got to where they are. Find out about their spending and saving habits. Begin to emulate the parts that sound attractive to you and watch what happens. Most people are thrilled to give advice—it makes them feel seen and valued. Don't be shy, give it a whirl!

Move Toward Growth

The other way to improve your cast of characters is to start from the inside out. Take your own journey toward growth and happiness, and the people around you who are no longer helpful for your path will begin to drop away. Warning: this can be painful! Your current cast of characters may not be able to handle the new and improved you. Some may have liked you better before you started getting all positive and self-actualized and shit. Sadly, they may like you better when you're weak and confused than when you have a clear purpose and feel empowered. They may not feel needed by you any more, or your forward movement could threaten their security in the relationship and in themselves. Be prepared for what Martha Beck calls "change-back attacks," in which the cohorts who were comfortable with you just the way you were consciously or unconsciously sabotage your attempts to evolve.

While this is hard, I want to reassure you that you will find new people who will propel your journey of growth in a way that will have you wondering why you were ever OK in the situation you left. It can be a bit like when you look at a photo of yourself in an outfit you wore ten years ago and you cannot believe you thought you looked smokin' hot in that get-up. It fit who you were at the time, but now it just doesn't express you anymore. I love the saying "Friends are either for a reason, a season, or a lifetime." Everyone isn't meant to accompany you from birth to death, and that's OK.

Please know that I am not suggesting you disown all of your friends or family who are having a hard time, sick, scared, poor, or temporarily out of sorts. I am also not advocating that you hitch your wagon to the brightest star you can find. This is not about using people to advance your personal agenda. Absolutely not! It's about learning from mentors and guides along the way—and when the time is right, you can pay it forward!

Want more MOJO? Find people who have the MOJO you desire and study them. Feel what it's like to be in their energy. Talk with them about their philosophy of life, or on their particular brand of MOJO—and new groups of friends will open up to you that you never knew existed. It's worth the effort, I promise!

MOJO in Motion...

Take stock of the five people you spend the most time with. List them here:

1) _____
2) _____
3) _____
4) _____
5) _____

What do you like about them?

_____

How do they support your growth?

_____

What do you dislike?

_____

Do they contribute to your MOJO deficit? How?

_____

Then take an honest look inward and determine what you like and don't like about yourself. Be brave and go on about the business of changing what doesn't work for you anymore.

"Before you diagnose yourself with depression or low self-esteem, first make sure you are not, in fact, surrounded by assholes."

~ William Gibson

Chapter 22:
MOJO Killer #15
Depression

"That's the thing about depression: A human being can survive almost anything, as long as she sees the end in sight. But depression is so insidious, and it compounds daily, that it's impossible to ever see the end. The fog is like a cage without a key."

~ Elizabeth Wurtzel, "Prozac Nation"

Depression is no joke. It's not weakness, and it's not lack of appreciation of life. It's a real disorder that affects you in ways you can't imagine if you've never experienced it yourself. It's an unrelenting sadness that sucks your soul, crushes your spirit, and makes you forget the greatness of who you are. Investigate the difference between having a bout of the blues and clinical depression. The antidote to the blues is connection and actively rejecting isolation. But if it's the latter YOU NEED TREATMENT. **The antidote to true depression is proper treatment.**

I've been open about being treated for depression, though most people would never imagine the pain I've hidden behind a smile. Luckily, I've found really helpful strategies that keep depression in remission.

If you are struggling with depression, *please keep seeking treatment until something works.* And something WILL work—don't give up. There is hope.

It's Chemistry, Not Character

First of all, if you are not functioning well, or if it takes an inordinate amount of energy to get even the smallest task accomplished, be open to the possibility of medication. Be evaluated by a psychiatrist—that's their specialty. If you don't like the first one you see, go see a different one. The first medication you try may not work; I had to try several before I got one that worked well.

In my opinion, untreated depression is much worse than most of the possible side effects from medication. In fact, untreated depression is not only a MOJO Killer: it can kill your spirit, crush your libido, and it can even take your life. Remember, depression is a flaw in chemistry, not character.

Your body can't heal when you are depressed. That should tell us how debilitating depression is physically. And you don't necessarily have to be on antidepressants forever. When you are stabilized, you can consider how long staying on medication is right for you. Sometimes it's for a few months, maybe a few years, possibly for the rest of your life.

Yes, Therapy

Second, get therapy. Deal with the shit you've been repressing your entire life. Take it out, look at it, and feel your feelings. Again, you've got to feel it to heal it. The fear of dealing with it is far worse than actually dealing with it, I promise you. You don't have to lie on a couch for forty years contemplating your belly button or blaming your parents and everyone you ever met. I don't want you to dwell in regret or blame yourself either. Try a large and regular dose of self-compassion instead. Becoming whole isn't about placing blame—but we do need to take responsibility for our healing because no one else will do it for us.

Learn Good Mental Hygiene

When you are good and sick of your own story, possibly try coaching. Coaching works because it teaches you good mental health hygiene. A good coach will teach you to question your negative thoughts, help you to bust through limiting beliefs, build your confidence by helping you discover your strengths, and serve as a trusted guide for your personal and professional growth. Having a trained coach in your corner can facilitate healing and success on every level.

Learn what your depression triggers are and develop strategies to combat them. Here are some of mine:

- I don't watch the news. It's a distorted view of the world—focusing on the negative and magnifying it to astronomical proportions. Our nervous systems are not made to handle the details of every single heinous atrocity committed on every corner of the globe.
- I make sure I eat well, and sleep enough.
- I don't hang out with people who treat me badly or make me doubt my sanity—even if they are family.
- I protect my energy like the Queen guards the crown jewels.
- I infuse my life with positivity.

When you are depressed, you can't remember what makes you feel better, so have something readily available.

Here are some things you can do to put your MOJO in motion:

- Put together a box where you put in a note about every single thing you remember that makes you happy.
- Have a happy music playlist.
- Learn to detach from painful thought patterns that create suffering.

- Practice random acts of kindness,
- Read good news, cuddle with pets, go for a walk, spend time in the sunshine for vitamin D. Make yourself go to gatherings where you feel loved.
- Don't retreat; keep involving yourself in life.
- Do things that feed your spirit.
- Most of all, treat depression as the serious disorder that it is. Medicate it if you need to and don't be ashamed of it.

Being depressed does not make you weak or ungrateful. I'll never forget when I went on medication and I was doing some self-shaming about "needing" it. I asked my sister what people did before antidepressants, and she said, "They drank, Keisha. Take the meds."

When In Doubt, Have it Checked Out

If you are wondering if you're depressed, please take a depression symptom screening online and then talk to your doctor. Depression doesn't always look like what you think. I used to think that it looked like someone unable to function that doesn't shower, brush their teeth, or get out of bed. Most people with depression do all of those things, but everything feels like a big huge effort. It can look like being irritable, feeling more negative, or even being a little paranoid. You may feel withdrawn and not want to socialize with people you've previously enjoyed. You may feel like "no one wants to talk to me because I have nothing good to say." You may have difficulty seeing a future for yourself or a solution to any of your problems. You may even be in a lot of physical pain that you can't really attribute to anything in particular. You may be self-medicating with drugs or alcohol or slipping back into self-destructive bad habits. Notice if your sleep or eating patterns have shifted recently, and check your level of feeling overwhelmed by things that in the past felt doable but now feel very difficult. Feeling like you are in a cloud or experiencing muddy thinking is really common with depression.

If you feel like you might have something going on, it doesn't hurt to have it checked out—and don't stop seeking help until you feel seen and heard by a professional. You deserve to feel better, so don't give up.

Chapter 23:
How to Get Your MOJO On

"Faith is taking the first step even when
you can't see the whole staircase. "
~ *Martin Luther King, Jr.*

Once you realize you've lost your MOJO, getting it back could be quite a challenge…IF you didn't have this book—which you do, so NO WORRIES! We've got this!

What you've got to do is go back to a time when you remember having MOJO. We need to go on a MOJO-mining expedition.

Jack was an investment banker, smart and calculating—his mind actually works like a computer. At work, he was always praised and revered for his ability to keep calm under pressure—a cool cucumber. His day consisted of trading millions of dollars in the blink of an eye. No pressure there, right? He was recognized for constantly assessing risk, looking at the next step, and deducing the least risky way to get the biggest gain. After Jack had excelled at his job for fifteen very successful years, the company he worked for closed its doors. Jack was thrown into a tailspin—the proverbial golden child's MOJO took a dirt nap when he lost his job.

The investment banking industry was radically changed by the global financial crisis, so Jack decided not to pursue a similar position in a new area. Instead, he took a job that was heavy on schmoozing and "working your contacts." It required behaving in ways that felt forced and disingenuous to him. He missed the camaraderie of his buddies at the trading desk, because his new job's social environment consisted of Jack alone in his office, on the phone trying to set up meetings. There was a lack of guidance and non-existent training, which made him feel alone and frankly, unsuccessful. Feeling like a square peg forced into a round hole, Jack hired me to help him find a new career.

Being the logical and strategic thinker that he is, Jack began assessing his options in a detached manner that made me queasy. There's no MOJO in detachment! I suggested instead that he ponder the idea of his next career move based on the excitement and passion he felt when picturing himself in a particular field. However, the idea that he could make a decision based on how he feels rather than what the stats say was foreign to him. Turns out that in the process of becoming such a high-achieving employee at his last job, Jack had lost touch with his feelings.

Jack had also forgotten how intuitively he had worked while making split second decisions at the trading desk. I explained to him that his magic was in the place where his computer brain and his intuition met—it was such a fantastic combination before, and now he just had to harness that chemistry to use in his next endeavor.

I asked Jack to tell me something he was once really good at that he had stopped doing. He told me he was a very talented artist as a kid—he had won awards and was in advanced placement art classes. It always felt like a hobby to him, though—nothing that he would ever use to make money. So he stopped drawing when he began his career as an investment banker. What was the point of drawing? It was just a silly time killer, and he had felt there was no purpose in wasting valuable time doing something for no discernible benefit.

I asked Jack to draw anything he wanted for one hour and let me know how it went when he came for our next session. He looked at me like I just told him to go to the North Pole and check out the progress Santa was making on his toy building. I explained to him that we were going to put him into a new mindset that remembered what it felt like to know what the hell he was doing, and to feel good about it. He needed to stop the internal downward spiral that his life had become since losing his beloved career and get the first inkling of traction that leads to MOJO.

The drawings that Jack brought to our next

appointment were excellent, and I saw an excitement in him that was new. He suddenly began telling me about a series of ideas he had for products he wanted to create—all wildly different, but equally intriguing. Jack's ideas came when he was using all of his strongest skills—drawing (design), intuition (creativity), and logical problem solving (how to make his ideas come to life in the real world). Right now he is in the process of launching his first product, and I have no doubt there will be many more to come. Allowing himself to play and rediscover a "hobby" that he loved as a kid sparked Jack's MOJO and set him on a whole new career path!

Finding Your MOJO

The first step to finding your MOJO is engaging in a task or skill that feels easy and fun. We love to do things that we're good at—it makes us feel confident. There's a reason why little kids always want to read the same book when they are learning to read—they know how to read it and it feels good to repeat what they know. It is only after a while of returning to the same well that something we've mastered gets boring, and we then set out to find a challenge.

When everything feels like a challenge because we've lost our MOJO, we need to go back to doing things we find easy—to use a skill that we take for granted because it feels like breathing to us, but not to everyone else.

If you loved to swim as a kid, go do some laps. If you

loved hiking, get out in nature and hoof it!

If you loved cooking, whittling, LEGO building, running, juggling, skateboarding or dancing—DO THAT! Do it now.

Notice how it feels to do that thing you do, notice how the muscle memory kicks right in. Notice how your brain quiets down and you feel a low hum in your body, as if to say, "Oh, yes—I remember you! I was hoping we'd do this again!"

I gave this assignment to one of my clients who had been a track star until she was injured. She cried as she told me how much she missed running—and that she could remember what it felt like to feel so light and carefree when she ran. But since her injury, after only ten minutes of running, the pain comes back and completely depresses her. So I told her to run for five minutes, and five minutes only.

Why bother only running for five minutes? Because it's better to do something you love for five minutes than to not do it at all. Especially when it gets your MOJO momentum going. If you physically can't indulge in your favorite pastime, find something that gives you the same feelings. My client could have taken up cycling or skinny-dipping to get the same light and carefree feeling she was missing. She found that engaging in this type of physical activity got her out of her head where she spent a lot of time plotting and strategizing (spinning and angsting) and into her body where she could take action and have more fun—ergo, MOJO.

MOJO in Motion...

If you didn't get it from the above story, I'll spell it out again; figure out what you loved to do as a kid and do it! ASAP! No excuses. It may seem silly or unrelated to your future goals, but don't let that stop you. MOJO doesn't follow rules! It follows what feels good!

Mining for MOJO

This Mining for MOJO meditation will help you to see what gems lie inside of you. It was adapted from a similar meditation that Mary Welty-Dapkus and I created for the Intuitive Gym.

Picture yourself as one of the seven dwarves, going down to work in the mine. There are precious gems in there, just waiting for you to pluck them from the earth. Now internalize that. Imagine that you are the mine—full of gems hoping to be excavated and brought into the light of day. Settle in to your heart and notice the gems—the qualities that lie in your heart. Allow the gems to speak to you and tell you what they are. Watch them emerge from your heart and into your consciousness. What precious resources do you possess that have yet to be mined? How can you better leverage these gems?

_____

_____

Chapter 24:
The Next Steps: Lock Up Your Inner Bully

*"It's not what you say out of your mouth that determines your life, it's
what you whisper to yourself that has the most power."*
~ Robert Kiyosaki

Now that you've found out which MOJO killers are
holding you back, you need to think about what else is
preventing you from accessing your MOJO. And I'm
here to tell you it's that little voice in your head—and
that voice has been with you since you were a kid.

We've all had the delightful pleasure of encountering
a bully in our youth. You may have even been her prey.

Due to my dad's career as a corporate climber, I
was the new girl every couple of years, and my arrival
made me fresh meat for the resident bullies at each new
school.

The worst part was that I was NICE—actually
pretending to ignore their hateful remarks and rude

stares. I was taught to "kill them with kindness." That if I just ignored them, they would get tired of picking on me and leave me alone. That actually didn't work any better than trying to gently pet a rabid dog. I think it just made me easy pickins.

Thankfully I went on to college, where I felt fully accepted and appreciated for my uniqueness, and the road from there on out was so much easier.

Well, in the outside world, but not in my own head.

See, each bully seemed to morph all of her most obnoxious traits into a shrew stew, which gave birth to my own INNER bully—a wretched bitch if I may say so, who has something nasty to say about a lot of the things I feel, say, do, or wear.

If you were unfortunate enough to have family members who liked to kick your self-esteem around for sport, add their nasty voices to the scrum as well. Psychologists call this identifying with your abuser. It's how our ego defends itself—the abuser doesn't feel as threatening if we believe what they tell us. It's like, "We're all on the same side!" Yeah, all on the side of shaming the victim—and this is not good! It's like if your grandma told you that you're stupid and ugly and that no man would ever want you, and then twenty years after she's dead you are still hearing her words in your head and accepting them as gospel truth. (I'll give grandma the benefit of the doubt and say that she "was looking out for our best interests" when she said that mean shit, but usually put-downs are a function of a bruised ego projecting its own issues onto someone else.)

As we grow and become socialized, somehow all those bullying words from others turn into our own internal voice, and we end up talking to ourselves in the same way. We even fool ourselves into thinking we need that mean voice, and that it's actually for our own good. We think we need the inner bully to protect us from eating that brownie so we won't get fat, from making that mistake at work, or from embarrassing ourselves by trying something new. But really, that nasty bully keeps us from accessing our MOJO. It stops us from being ourselves and SHAMES us, which is not productive at all.

*Important note— your inner bully is NOT your conscience, and it's not your intuition. As I've said before, your intuition speaks in a neutral, levelheaded manner. Your conscience sounds like Jiminy Cricket— not Simon Cowell.

In response to this, I propose a revolt. Yes, I want you to lock up your inner bully. Just shut that bitch up! Here's how.

INVESTIGATE HER

- Keep a log of her put-downs for a day.
- What's her MO?
- What does she say?
- When does she strike?
- What provokes her?

PICK HER OUT OF A LINEUP

- Go back to the scene of the crime—in this case—your own slanderous remark. Where have you heard that voice before? Does it sound familiar?
- Your inner bully is usually just a copycat, picking up where the real bully left off.

*Remember—you don't have to believe every thought that goes through your mind!

- Stop her in her tracks.
- Draw a composite sketch of the perp.
- Give her a name.

Now we are separating her from you, which makes it much easier to squelch her without remorse.

PUT HER ON TRIAL

Does she tell the truth, the whole truth, and nothing but the truth, so help her God? 100% of the time? Do you really look like an elephant in those jeans? Are you truly the stupidest person who ever lived? Totally incompetent? The worst [insert name] on the planet?

Yeah, I didn't think so. Bullies lie. They lie to make themselves feel better because they feel woefully inadequate. So, believing her story is like believing every doomsday whack job that says the world is ending next week.

You could continue going ahead and listening to that looney tune, but in the past her insults have probably led you to deplete your savings, rack up a boatload of credit card debt, get in relationships with people who treat you poorly, smoke a pack a day, or eat an entire cheesecake in one sitting…right? All because you've been listening to a delusional nut case with a ridiculous ego and believing her lies.

SEND HER TO THE SLAMMER

If prison sounds harsh, call it "reform school" and assuage your guilt. Picture your bully in a very institutional time-out at the detention facility of your choice. Tell her it's time for her to take care of her own mess and move on. It's justifiable self-defense.

REHABILITATE YOURSELF

The time for self-inflicted pain is over. As part of your rehabilitation process, you must learn to love each scar, each vulnerability, each "imperfection." After all, perfection is passé—it's boring, unattainable, and lacks character.

I implore my clients who are going through a very difficult time to take care of themselves as they would a small child. This usually registers a degree of shock on their faces, not because the idea sounds ludicrous, but because it makes them realize how unkindly they've been treating themselves.

SET YOURSELF FREE

You are now free to look at yourself as you would a baby in a nursery. Are there any "unworthy" babies there? Any babies who would be perfect if they would just stop being so lazy, stupid, or unlovable? Of course not—what kind of a lunatic would think such a thing?

It's no different for adults. Just because our meat suits (bodies) have cellulite, wrinkles, or hairy backs doesn't mean we are no longer just as worthy as we were the day we were born. Each of us is a magnificent creation, filled with amazing capabilities and endless possibility. So, the next time you hear that bully spew something toxic, tell her to zip it or else. As Martha Beck says, "Self loathing is so 20th-century."

It's a new age—give your inner bully up to the feds and watch your self-esteem soar.

MOJO in Motion...

To get rid of your inner bully, you have to notice each and every time she shows up to torment you.

Thank her for showing up, but tell her you no longer wish to hear from her. You'll be surprised at how quickly she stops coming to play when she knows you won't fall into the pit of despair she is digging for you.

Chapter 25:
Change Your Mindset

"Whether you think you can, or you think you can't—you're right."
~ Henry Ford

Once you have reignited a long-lost love by doing something that you're really good at, mined your MOJO for gems, and locked up your inner bully, you are ready for the next step.

Fake it 'Til You Make It

You know how good it feels to have passion for something? To feel a heightened awareness in your body so that what you're doing feels virtually effortless and on track with your purpose? Well, you can channel that same kind of ease even toward activities you might not usually think of as your "passion." As Philip Stanhope once said, "Whatever is worth doing at all is worth doing well."

So experiment with applying this kind of passion to doing something ordinary. I heard Oprah say that when she makes her bed (on the weekends when she doesn't have help), she pretends she is Martha Stewart making a bed. Do you find that as funny as I do? Not only is the thought of Oprah Winfrey pretending to be anyone else hilarious, so is envisioning her make her own bed. But I understand why she does it; she is inserting reverence into an everyday chore by giving her all to a ho-hum task.

I've done this with cooking—which I hate. But if I listen to Andrea Bocelli and get a glass of wine while I cook pasta, I start feeling like I'm Giada De Laurentiis. All of a sudden, I feel more creative and inspired to put a little love and zest into a routine duty that a minute ago felt like drudgery.

Yes, my friends, this is a case of "fake it 'til you make it." When we're trying to increase our MOJO, we want to gain momentum. Good momentum. And you don't need to do something superhuman to gain momentum, just begin where you are. When you can connect to that feeling of mastery, no matter what you're doing, it brings about feelings of positivity and focus, two main ingredients of MOJO.

Establishing a Growth Mindset

This is a process of getting into the right frame of mind. Stanford professor Carol Dweck, PhD, wrote a book called *Mindset: The New Psychology of Success* in which she talks about the power of having a growth mindset rather than a fixed mindset. When we have a growth mindset, we focus on the challenge of a problem and dedicate ourselves to persevering rather than giving up. If we approach things from a fixed mindset, we limit ourselves by thinking we can't expand our capacity for growth because we're as smart as we're ever going to be—after all, you can't teach an old dog a new trick, right? Wrong! Research shows that the brain has neuroplasticity and can be molded and expanded when effort is applied. We can literally rewire our brains for more MOJO!

Here is how Dweck recommends switching from a fixed to a growth mindset:

Learn to identify your fixed mindset in action by listening to the voice in your head—your inner bully. It will tell you that you can't do it and shouldn't try, to play it safe, and to avoid ridicule. Charming, eh?

Realize you have a choice in how you think about success and failure. You can make a decision to adapt a growth mindset. We are not our thoughts. Ever seen the bumper sticker that says, "Don't believe everything you think"? It means that we are the observer of our thoughts, not the thought itself. You are the consciousness that watches the thoughts go by. (If you want to know more about this concept, read Eckhart Tolle's *A New Earth* or *The Untethered Soul* by Michael A. Singer.) Thoughts continually come in and out of our minds like debris. Don't attach to every thought you think. First ask yourself if it's helpful. If it is empowering, keep it. If it is defeating, ditch it.

Talk back to your fixed mindset with a growth-mindset voice. Have a turnaround thought ready for when you hear doubts about your ability to conquer a new challenge, learn a new skill, or persevere in the face of failure. Yes, this means you will be pumping sunshine up your own ass on a regular basis. And that's OK! New research shows that we perform better on tasks when we speak to ourselves using our first name (yes, in the third person) as if we are talking to a friend. As in, "Laura, you can totally make it through the last ten minutes of this heinous spin class. You are awesome!" How we talk to ourselves is critical to our self-perception—and now there's evidence that it affects our performance as well.

Be your own coach—tell yourself that you are in the process of learning something you really want to learn, and that every day you are becoming more capable and more determined. Study success stories in which people have overcome seemingly insurmountable odds to succeed (like Michael Jordan, Thomas Edison, Walt Disney, etc.). My friend Kirsten just told me she went to high school with jazz singer Diana Krall, and that at the time Diana tried out for choir and didn't make it. She was an excellent piano player, but her voice was considered too low to be useful in choir. Now she has five Grammy awards, is married to singer/songwriter Elvis Costello, and is one of the most famous jazz artists in history. It's easy to think that some people just "have it" and we just don't—but there is no fundamental difference between us and them, only the fact that they've already made it!

People who have succeeded have also faced failure after failure—but they kept going, with no loss of enthusiasm or tenacity, overcoming the obstacles in their way. They never entertained the idea that they wouldn't complete their mission. It was just a matter of time.

Take the growth mindset action. Again and again and again.

Chapter 26:
Where Is Your MOJO Rockin'?

"I've got moves you've never seen."
~ Julia Roberts in "My Best Friend's Wedding"

Let's take a look at your MOJO level in the important areas of your life....

Please rate each category on a scale of 1–10 in terms of satisfaction level.

CAREER

How MOJO-full do you feel in your career? Are you doing something you love? Hell, are you doing something you even like? Or do you hate what you do almost every day of your life?

Rate yourself a "one" if you feel like an indentured servant, doing revolting work that you despise and that makes your time at work feel like a prison sentence.

"Ten" means you feel like a rock star, can't believe you get paid to do what you do, and are incredibly fulfilled. (If you're in between jobs at the moment, answer for the last position you had.)

1   2   3   4   5   6   7   8   9   10

Now, how would you rate the people you work with or the customers you interact with? One means you can't imagine what unforgivable crimes you committed in a past life to deserve working with these assholes, and ten means you love these people and cannot believe that such amazing people exist and you get to work with them.

1   2   3   4   5   6   7   8   9   10

Does your work feel meaningful? Like it makes a difference?

One means your mission feels like the dumbest, most inconsequential crap ever and if your job went away tomorrow, who the hell would care? Ten means, "Holy cow! I feel like what I do is very important to the people I know and interact with. Without people like me doing what I do, the world would really miss out."

1   2   3   4   5   6   7   8   9   10

Do you feel you get to use your strengths and talents in a rewarding way in your work? One means that no part of your essential self shows up at this crappy job or that you're completely misplaced in the position you're in. Ten means you get to use your favorite skills and biggest talents in a creative way most of the time.

1   2   3   4   5   6   7   8   9   10

Do you feel your time is used well at work? One means you spend most of your time doing things that are a complete waste of time and ten means you feel fully engaged in high-priority items most of the time.

1   2   3   4   5   6   7   8   9   10

Do you feel you are compensated well for the time and effort you put into your work? Do you feel you have good benefits or perks? One means, "I can hardly live on what I make...and by the way, what are perks and benefits?" Ten means, "Oh my gosh, can you believe I get to write this off and call it work?" or "I cannot believe that someone will pay me this much money to do what is right up my alley and that I would probably do for free!"

1   2   3   4   5   6   7   8   9   10

Overall, do you feel your work is an extension of you and your mission in this life? Is it fun? Are you challenged?

1   2   3   4   5   6   7   8   9   10

RELATIONSHIPS

How MOJO-full do you feel in your relationships? Do you have a tight-knit group of friends you can count on for support, understanding, and companionship? Do you have a life partner you are in love with? Do you like who you are in your relationships?

Where would you rate your level of satisfaction of your friendships on a scale of one-ten? One means, "What friendships?" or "Oh, you mean those backstabbers who say they're my friends?" and ten means, "I could not have picked more fantastic people to put in my life—they always have my back, we have fun together, and they really get me."

1   2   3   4   5   6   7   8   9   10

If you have a friendship or two that's mucking up your friendship satisfaction level, what's the problem with that relationship?

_____

Does this relationship feel evenly matched and have give and take on both sides? Do you feel loyalty and good energy coming toward you from this relationship? Do you feel understood or lifted up when in this person's company?

If not, why do you continue to invest or hang onto this friendship?

_____

_____

Where would you rate your love relationship if you have one? One means, "I may as well be alone, because I'm already alone" or "Being in this marriage is making me physically ill." Ten means, "This person is made for me! I couldn't have designed a more perfect relationship because we are crazy in love, I feel deeply supported and understood, and we complement and challenge one another's growth." (If you just threw up a little in your mouth, don't worry—you are not alone!)

1   2   3   4   5   6   7   8   9   10

If you have a less-than-stellar relationship with your spouse or significant other—what's the problem? Don't feel connected? Feel disrespected? Feel resentful? Having no fun? Going in different directions? Power struggles?

What keeps you going in this relationship? Why are you still there?

_____

_____

What about your relationships with your family? Parents, sisters or brothers, children? One means, "I have a terrible relationship with my parents and it is stressful speaking to or spending time with any of my family," and ten means, "I feel totally thrilled with my family relationships because I feel supported, cared for, and connected, and I am incredibly thankful to have been born into this family."

Parents
1   2   3   4   5   6   7   8   9   10

Sisters or Brothers
1   2   3   4   5   6   7   8   9   10

Children
1   2   3   4   5   6   7   8   9   10

What's mucking up your relationships with your family?

_____

What's making your family relationships strong?

How about your relationship with yourself—do you speak to yourself the way you would speak to someone you care about, or does your inner bully have control of the conversation? Do you think kind and compassionate thoughts, or is your head a scary neighborhood? One means, "I would never allow anyone to speak to me the way I speak to me," and ten means, "I have learned to use kind words and much less judgment when I speak to myself. I talk to myself as I would to someone I love."

1   2   3   4   5   6   7   8   9   10

HEALTH

How healthy do you feel on a scale of one to ten?

One means, "I am sick and tired of being so sick and tired—my lack of health totally blocks my MOJO," and ten means, "I love my body, how it works, and what it does!"

1   2   3   4   5   6   7   8   9   10

Do you like how your body looks? One means, "I want a refund!" and ten means, "I wouldn't trade this body for the world!"

1   2   3   4   5   6   7   8   9   10

Are you able to do the things you want to do with the body you have? One means, "I think I got a lemon—who do I talk to about that?" and ten means, "I can do anything I want in my body, and I am so grateful!"

1   2   3   4   5   6   7   8   9   10

Do you exercise your body regularly in a way that feels like fun, not punishment? One means, "Does walking to the vending machine count?" and ten means, "I attend the best exercise class! I look forward to it and it's so much fun!"

1   2   3   4   5   6   7   8   9   10

Do you feed your body healthy food? One means, "If it doesn't come in a box, I'm not eating it," and ten means, "I love eating real, whole foods with lots of color and tons of nutrition."

1   2   3   4   5   6   7   8   9   10

Do you drink alcohol responsibly, or has it become a crutch or an addiction? One means, "I pollute my body every chance I get," and ten means, "I drink in moderation or rarely," or "I gave that up and it's the best thing I ever did."

1   2   3   4   5   6   7   8   9   10

Do you use prescription or over-the-counter medications responsibly? Do you use recreational drugs, or abuse prescription drugs? One means, "I feel like Keith Richards, I'm surprised I'm still alive," and ten means, "I use all drugs sparingly and wisely."

1   2   3   4   5   6   7   8   9   10

Do you go to a health care provider regularly for check-ups and screenings to prevent disease? One means, "I hang a rope of garlic around my neck and hope for the best because you can't trust the medical establishment!" and ten means, "I make a point to stay on top of my health with excellent professional care."

1   2   3   4   5   6   7   8   9   10

Do you pamper yourself with health-promoting practices such as massage, Reiki treatments, facials, saunas, yoga, and meditation? One means, "What the hell kind of new-age hippy-dippy shit are you talking about?" and ten means, "I engage in self-care regularly for my mind, body, and spirit."

1   2   3   4   5   6   7   8   9   10

MONEY

How is your money MOJO working? Do you respect money? How do you demonstrate that?

_____

_____

Do you feel you have enough money? One means, "Not only am I broke, I owe more money than I can ever pay back," and ten means, "Money loves me; I've got more than enough."

1   2   3   4   5   6   7   8   9   10

Do you feel you are fairly compensated for the work you do? Do you earn enough money to have the lifestyle you want?

_____

_____

Do you save money monthly? Do you have a robust savings account? Do you contribute to your retirement? One means, "What part of broke don't you understand? I can't save money I don't have!" and ten means, "I could retire right now if I wanted to—I'm set for life!"

1   2   3   4   5   6   7   8   9   10

Do you like the way you spend money? Do the things you spend money on feel like the best use of your money? One means, "All my money goes down a rat hole and I have nothing to show for it," and ten means, "I spend money according to my values and I feel gratitude for the things I am able to buy."

1   2   3   4   5   6   7   8   9   10

Do you give money away to worthwhile causes that align with your values? When you send that money off does it feel fantastic? Do you feel blessed when you contribute to a person or organization that uses your funds wisely? One means, "I can't remember the last time I gave money away" or "I donate someplace I feel I'm supposed to rather than where I'd really like to," and ten means, "Giving money away is a pure pleasure and something I do regularly and to places I feel good about."

1   2   3   4   5   6   7   8   9   10

When you think about money, where are you on the fear and joy spectrum? One means, "I have a constant fear of not having enough money; I worry about it constantly and I talk about it all the time," and ten means, "I love money— it brings me joy, I always have enough—I'm a money magnet!"

1   2   3   4   5   6   7   8   9   10

SPIRITUALITY

Do you feel in touch with your complete MOJO-ness as a result of your connection to spirit? One means, "Um, what the hell are you talking about?" and ten means, "I feel connected to the Universe, source, and everything in it—which makes me feel awesome and loved!"

1   2   3   4   5   6   7   8   9   10

Do you have a spiritual practice that fulfills you? One means, "Um, seriously—what the hell are you talking about?" and ten means, "I have lots of ways that I practice that I can rely on to help me feel connected to something bigger than myself."

1   2   3   4   5   6   7   8   9   10

Do you have a group of like-minded people who share your vision of spirituality? Do they support and enhance your growth process? One means, "Wait, that's a thing?" and ten means, "Oh yeah, I've got lots of that going on—how did I ever survive without them?"

1   2   3   4   5   6   7   8   9   10

Do you make time to seek answers to spiritual questions through prayer, meditation, clergy, spiritual mentors, books, or workshops? One means, "Um, again...what the hell are you talking about?" and ten means, "I have a plethora of resources I call upon to become closer to God, the Universe, source, or spirit..."

1   2   3   4   5   6   7   8   9   10

Do you have a faith or philosophy that sustains you when your mind wonders why things happen as they do? One means, "You mean like, 'Life sucks and then you die?'" and ten means, "Yes, that's what keeps me sane!"

1   2   3   4   5   6   7   8   9   10

JOY

How happy do you feel most of the time? One means, "I can't remember the last time I had FUN," and ten means, "I'm a one-woman party—I feel an immense amount of joy daily!"

1   2   3   4   5   6   7   8   9   10

When do you feel the happiest? A certain time of day? Are there certain activities that light you up?

_____

_____

What are some things you could do more of to create more joy in your life?

_____

_____

How can you allow more joy into your life? Where are you holding yourself back from joy?

_____

_____

Do you laugh easily and often? One means, "I rarely laugh out loud—I could be a guard at Buckingham Palace, no problem," and ten means, "I get the giggles at the slightest provocation—don't even think about bringing me to church or a library!"

1   2   3   4   5   6   7   8   9   10

Do you have a feeling of deep passion for any person, place, thing, or activity? One means, "I'm not sure what passionate means, but I'm fairly certain if I had it, I'd know it," and ten means, "I've got so many passions I can barely keep up—I'm a passionate lover of life!"

1   2   3   4   5   6   7   8   9   10

Do you feel creative? Do you like to make things, write, grow, learn? One means, "I am a total creature of habit; I have been doing the same things the same way every day for as long as I can remember," and ten means, "I make it a point to learn new things, and I go for creative solutions to any issue I encounter!"

1   2   3   4   5   6   7   8   9   10

Do you try new things? Challenge yourself to go outside your comfort zone? Are you willing to completely suck at something you'd like to eventually do well? One means, "The last new thing I tried was sushi in 2003—I barfed all night and have been eating a steady diet of beige food ever since," and ten means, "I try new things all the time and I am willing to look like a fool" or "I embarrass my children with my spontaneous eruptions of dorkiness regularly!"

1   2   3   4   5   6   7   8   9   10

Do you hang out with people who bring you joy? Is your social circle a positive and uplifting one? One means, "Who needs enemies when I've got these cynical douchebags to 'brighten my day?'" and ten means, "My buddies are pure rays of sunshine!"

1   2   3   4   5   6   7   8   9   10

Do you have pets that bring you joy?

_____

_____

What do you do for others that brings joy to all involved?

_____

_____

How can you be more deliberate about creating and allowing more joy and FUN into your life?

_____

_____

How's your sex life? Are you stimulated and excited about sexual activity, or does this area of your life need a serious makeover? One means, "Ummmm, I'm not really a sexual person, so basically, I live like a eunuch," and ten means, "I could give classes on how to embrace your sexuality and I would be an instant zillionaire!"

1   2   3   4   5   6   7   8   9   10

Now that you've rated your MOJO in the critical areas of your life, go back and look at where you need to concentrate. Anywhere you've got a score of five or lower, you know you've gotta go there. What's missing? What needs to happen? Close your eyes and really listen to your heart. It knows.

_____

_____

Score of 6–8? Doing great! What little steps could you make to boost that score even hire? Little tweaks can make a big difference!

Score of 9 or 10? You could write this book. You are a volcano of hot molten MOJO! Do your happy dance and give yourself a parade! WOOHOO! Whatever you're doing, keep at it!

Casey's
MOJO Story

Talented giggler, Tenacious change-
maker, my new MOJO idol

Casey is a hilarious woman with the best, most
contagious laugh I've ever heard. Sadly, she used to hide
a lot of suffering behind that fun-loving personality.
Casey came to me looking to revamp her entire life.
Her recent tennis coaching experience had made such
a huge difference in her tennis game that she thought
hiring a life coach might do the same for her life.

Casey was feeling crappy about her work as a manager
at a large corporation—burned out, frustrated, and
uninspired. Her romantic relationship was unsatisfying
to say the least and unraveling fast. At the forefront
of Casey's issues was her weight—she had lost and

regained the same one-hundred pounds several times over and was completely despondent over how she had let the weight creep back over time (not coincidentally, as her relationship was falling apart). When I met her, she was depressed and retreating from the world.

Casey began to open up about the struggles with weight that had been present her entire life, giving me more and more information as she began to trust me. I learned that she had tried several medically supervised weight loss programs to no avail. She tossed out the idea of gastric bypass surgery as taking the "easy way out."

I responded to her by saying, "What's wrong with taking the easy way out?" The question hit her right between the eyes. Why was it wrong to take the easy way out?

Now first of all, there is nothing easy about gastric bypass surgery. It is successful in the majority of patients, but can cause serious complications or even be fatal. It was not covered by her insurance and it was expensive. She would miss work for several weeks and had to decide what she was going to tell her coworkers about why she was gone. So, definitely NOT easy. And secondly, even if it WAS the easy way out…so what? Yo-yo dieting over her life span was taking a toll on her health and eviscerating Casey's self confidence—this was as permanent a fix as she was going to find. Why not do things the easy way when there's an easier way available? You don't get a medal for doing everything the hardest, most painful way you can, do you? That's martyrdom and I am not a fan.

Casey needed to call upon her MOJO to make a decision about whether to have this weight loss surgery. She wanted to make her weight loss permanent and she knew how much being heavy was limiting how she was living her life. Together we envisioned her as the fit person she wanted to be and began brainstorming all the things she would do with a lighter, healthier body. Sports, travel, being social, and dating were all things that had a promising outlook if she weighed less.

We began listing all the physical things she wanted to be able to do that would be possible—improve her tennis game, zip line, and sky dive. We talked about all the places she wanted to go in the world that felt off-limits to her because of her lack of stamina and travel restrictions at her current weight. We talked about the loving partnership that was missing in her life because she was too afraid of rejection and thought she had to settle for whoever would have her.

Casey mustered her very adventurous spirit and took the first step by planning a consultation with a doctor and bringing a friend for support. She evoked her awesome sense of humor to confront the anxiety she felt over the procedure. Casey brought forth her creativity by scheduling the surgery over the holidays when her company shut down for two weeks. And she unleashed her determination to see this path through to success. There were a few complications during her surgery that caused her to miss a bit more work than she had planned, but she remained solid in her determination to ride out the difficult patches for a better future.

Four months after her surgery, Casey traveled to London and Rome and was able to keep up with a tour group. She had lost sixty pounds and was on track to lose fifty more. She signed up for a half marathon and trained throughout the summer to complete her goal of 13.1 miles. Since then, she's done three more, smaller races, "just to keep her fitness goals in check." She has also checked zip lining in Costa Rica off her bucket list and put her profile on a few dating sites. And last week she went skydiving! Casey sent me a picture of herself as she made her jump and the look of elation on her face makes my heart burst with joy!

Gone are the days of Casey staying home and self-medicating with food and wine. Today, at her goal weight, she is a vibrant woman who takes chances and is up for any adventure. She has become much more social, is taking classes just for the fun of it, and is finally becoming more comfortable in her skin. All of this newfound MOJO has also created success in her work because she's learned to advocate for herself against office bullies, and effectively manage the people who report to her who had mistaken her kindness for weakness. By creating the confidence to become more visible, she's increased her leadership capacity. Casey is on a serious roll, and I could not be happier for the opportunities she is creating for herself. All of this is possible now because Casey changed the self-defeating thinking that was keeping her stuck to empowered thinking that is propelling her toward action. She is one of my new MOJO idols!

Chapter 27:
Magnify Your MOJO

"The privilege of a lifetime is to become who you truly are."
~ Carl Jung

Now that you've looked at where your MOJO is rockin' and where it's not, let's see how we can magnify what's working and launch new MOJO where it's lagging. Good news! The ability to magnify your MOJO resides in you—not outside of you. You don't need luck, strategy, or positioning to get more MOJO; you don't need therapy or a facelift or tummy tuck either! You just need to look at the belief system that you knowingly and unknowingly subscribe to and untangle the unhelpful thoughts. You need to adapt a more positive outlook so you can take down the barriers that prevent you from being one with your MOJO.

Are you ready? Let's get crackin'!

Beliefs About Work

Let's look at your belief system when it comes to work. What you learned in childhood about what it is to work is ingrained in your psyche. It is governing how you think and act when it comes to your career. If you, like most people, learned that work is supposed to be hard and painful, and you still believe it, you will set up a life in which your work is hard and painful. It cannot be otherwise!

Even if somehow you have transcended your programming that work is hard and painful, and have nabbed an incredible job with money, benefits, and freedom galore—you may still make it hard for yourself to enjoy it because of the guilt you may feel about it NOT being painful enough.

Take Gilbert, a top salesman at a huge information technology firm. He called me because he said he needed a coach to help him get to the next level at his job. Turns out, he had exceeded his yearly sales quota *in January* but felt he still had room to grow, because he wanted to be the BEST.

Upon further examination, Gilbert was the kind of person who sets bigger and bigger goals for himself. That's great—I'm a coach, so I'm all about goals. But, when he accomplishes them, he only feels good about it for about three hours. The next day, he says: "Now what?" and sets an even bigger goal. Starting with a half marathon, then a full marathon, then a triathlon…he's running out of races to conquer.

The reason he can't keep that feeling of accomplishment is because he believes that work (of all sorts) is supposed to be hard. His mom was an incredibly driven, very successful businesswoman who instilled the belief that if you aren't working day and night feverishly to become better and better, then you're a slacker. Lazy, even.

Because of his disciplined behavior and great social skills, Gilbert was able to climb to the top of the ladder at every company he worked for, but each and every time, he became bored. One of the big reasons for that is that he doesn't know his WHY. Why is he working so hard? What does he stand for? Does his work feel meaningful to him? Gilbert has linked enjoyment with laziness and work with pain, so his life continues to reflect those beliefs.

It's heartbreaking to see someone with so much success unable to enjoy it.

Interestingly, but not surprisingly, Gilbert quit coaching with me after a few sessions because it "didn't seem challenging enough." He just didn't want to unhook from the belief that life was not to be enjoyed. He wanted a coaching dominatrix, someone who would whip him into shape by drilling and demanding that he do more and more, faster and harder dammit!!!! (I realize this sounds dirty, I'm just checking to see if you're paying attention.)

Plainly, I am just not that kind of coach. I am just heretical enough to say that I think you can enjoy your work, and that harder and faster does not make for better. We have the belief that anything worth doing is worth doing well, which is great! What's not great is thinking that the way we solve problems is by trying harder and doing it faster. This is a recipe for disaster, and losing your MOJO (or never truly finding it in the first place) is in your future if you keep approaching your problems this way.

The Power/Force Dynamic

There is a difference between power and force—and we always want to go with power. The power of what feels right to you will never steer you wrong. I can just hear you saying, "Wait, you want me to just go with what feels right? What if what feels right is curling up in a crack house with all my favorite junkies?" Nooo, your MOJO is not in drugs, or alcohol, gambling, illicit sex, or excessive shopping. Those things are outside of you, quick fixes that are temporary highs, leaving you empty and wanting more—all the while taking you further and further from your true North. They are distractions to keep you small and out of touch with your MOJO. We want you to embody your bigness. Not in stature, but in energy.

The way we do this is by playing a game of hot and cold with your life. When you're trying to make a decision about what direction to move in in your life (or any choice, really) you ask yourself—what feels better and what feels worse? And not in your thoughts—in your body. Your body is your subconscious mind. You can learn to pay attention to and follow the sensations you feel in your stomach, throat, chest, arms, legs, and big toe when you are in a situation that serves your MOJO, and also how your body feels when you are in one that sucks your MOJO.

The Body Compass

There is an unbelievable wealth of information for us in the sensations our bodies give us. There is a tool Martha Beck taught me in life coach training called "The Body Compass," and I teach it to EVERYONE who coaches with me because it's that powerful.

Here's how:

1. Sit or lie down comfortably and do a body scan of what your body feels like in a neutral state, starting from the bottom of your feet, then your ankles, shins, calves, knees, thighs, hips, belly, chest, heart, throat, collarbones, shoulders, biceps, elbows, forearms, hands, fingers, back, neck, over the top of your head, eyebrows, nose, mouth, and down into your jaw. You are just noticing—checking in with your body to say

"hello" to each body part, not trying to change anything. Notice any temperature, tightness, pain, or ease at each area of your body.

2. Imagine a really bad time you can remember in your life. I am not asking you to relive something terribly abusive or traumatic—we don't want this to be a trigger for a trauma response! Just something that was one of your more unpleasant experiences. It could be an upsetting argument, the end of a relationship, getting fired, or a scary diagnosis. (No it's not fun, but this serves a purpose, I promise, and we won't stay here for long.) Your mind will want to wrestle with which memory is the best for our purposes, but it doesn't matter which yucky memory you choose—just let one settle in and overtake you. Imagine you are watching this scene on a huge movie screen, and then jump in and really relive this experience. Make all of the visual details very crisp and vivid. Notice colors, facial expressions, and any details you can. Listen for tone of voice or music in the background. Do you smell or taste anything with this memory? Just notice what you notice.

3. Now, what do you feel in your body? How does your stomach feel? Your throat? Your chest? Your head? Jaw? Neck and shoulders? Arms and legs? Hands and feet? Do you notice any tension, pain, heaviness, or discomfort? Write down or record

yourself explaining the physical feelings you experience when you are reliving this memory.

4. Where would you rate this on a scale of zero to negative ten of all-time yucky feelings?

5. Let's give this icky feeling a name—something that you'll remember. I've heard everything from "purple" to "depression" to "Barstow." You are the only one who needs to know what you call the feeling; it's from your frame of reference.

6. Tell yourself that you are safe now and that you never have to revisit this memory again. Step out of the movie screen and watch the picture get smaller and smaller until it vanishes.

7. Open your eyes and literally shake it off. I want you to get up, move around, and physically shake your arms and legs and anything else you want to shake. Did you know that shaking is the body's way of processing trauma? It's what animals do when they are hurt, and what humans do when we go into shock. We want to mindfully shake off the negative feelings that are associated with reliving this negative time.

8. You have just learned what your body feels like when it doesn't like what's happening. This is your body's way of communicating with you so that you know when something is perceived as harmful to you and your MOJO. So, whenever you're in the midst of a job interview, a date, a meeting, putting an offer on a house—or anything

that requires you to make a decision—reach into your body and notice what you feel. Any twinge of one of the sensations you felt during this exercise is your body's way of saying NO, I don't like it. If you come out of a meeting and notice that your shoulders are up to your ears and you are in pain, that's a sign. If you meet someone and you have a vaguely sick feeling in your stomach, it's a sign. If you have an overall feeling of heaviness when trying to perform a task, it's a sign. Your body is telling you something—and you can trust it.

Now let's move on to learning when your body feels great. This is the fun part!

1. Repeat the steps from the body scan, going from your feet all the way up to your head. Notice anything tense, loose, hot, cold, comfortable, or uncomfortable.

2. Imagine a fantastic time in your life—one of the best memories you can conjure. Allow your mind to settle on one; don't worry if it's the best memory, any wonderful memory will do. See the memory on a big movie screen and then jump in and immerse yourself in this beautiful memory. Make sure all the details are vivid and crisp. Notice facial expressions, colors, and details. Listen for laughter, tone of voice, or music. Are there any smells or tastes associated with this

memory? If so, amp them up so you feel like you are actually there.

3. What do you feel in your body? Start with your stomach. What sensation do you feel? How about in your chest? Your heart? Notice your throat, your jaw, and your mouth. What do you notice in your neck and shoulders? Arms and legs?

4. Where would you rank this on a scale of zero to positive ten when it comes to feelings about great experiences you've had? How good do you feel?

5. Let's give this feeling a name, too—something you'll remember. Again, this is just for you, from your frame of reference. I've heard everything from "bubbles" to "honeymoon" to "light."

6. Go back to this feeling as often as possible! This is a keeper. It's something that will generate good feelings for you whenever you want them. Think of it as a tool you can use to get yourself into a good-feeling state at will.

Open your eyes and notice the feeling of wellbeing you are experiencing. You now know what your body feels like when it's saying, "Yes, more of this please!" This is your maximum MOJO state. Remember it and do anything that makes you feel even a teeny bit of what you're feeling in its fullest sense right now. People tell me they usually feel light, effervescent, relaxed, smiley, and expansive. Your posture will probably feel more open and you may stand up straighter when you feel this way.

It is possible for you to feel this way often! You can trust that this is your body's way of affirming that the activity you're engaged in is a good one for you, the person that you're with is one you can like, love, or trust, or this course of action is one that will intensify your MOJO!

To summarize—if a sensation feels bad in your body, it means something is wrong. You can trust it. Your body is receiving energetic information from the situation that feels bad and it is alerting you to the fact that something is not right! Learning about a new investment opportunity and your stomach feels sour and tight? Don't do it, even if it sounds good on paper. A friend calls and asks if he can come stay with you until he finds a job and your heart sinks and it feels like your feet are encased in cement? Find a kind way to say that you won't be able to help. You are not being a jerk by listening to your body compass and finding that it says HELL NO.

On the other hand, if you are interviewing for a job and you have a bubbly, excited feeling about it— pursue it with all your might! If helping a friend after surgery makes your heart feel warm—do it! If you're looking for the perfect house and you get a huge rush of good energy as you enter the front door of a particular dwelling, seriously consider buying it. Paying attention to these sensations will save you the painful work of un-fucking the consequences of a shitty decision made under pressure while trying to be nice and for someone else's good rather than your own. You can do it!!!

Chapter 28:
Concoct Your
MOJO Potion

"Recipe for success: Heat up an idea, take action, mix it up with
passion and belief, then add a dash of persistence."

~ *Unknown*

In this exercise, I'd like you to write down your particular concoction for your very best MOJO. It's a recipe—or a road map, so that if you lose your MOJO again, you know where to find it. Like Austin Powers, you discovered you had your MOJO all along!

Examples of a MOJO Potion

Keisha's MOJO Potion

Two heaping scoops of FUN
1/2 cup of sass mouth
3/4 cup of warm empathy
One dash of shameless truth serum
A few sprinkles of saucy language

(may substitute light-hearted mockery in a pinch)

Fold thoughtfully equal parts handholding and ass kicking while peppering with excellent, soul revealing inquiry. Marinate with love and understanding until sparkly and shiny. Dismount with a ridiculous happy dance and a rockin' action plan for world domination!

Casey's MOJO Potion

Remember Casey from earlier in the book? Remember how she used the MOJO-finding process to transform her entire life? Well, this is her own special MOJO concoction, and she invites you to partake of it liberally:

1 rounded cup of laughter + 1/4 cup of children's laughter

1/2 cup of tomfoolery or shenanigans (either is fine)

1/2 cup of creativity

Put all above ingredients in medium mixing bowl and stir well.

In a separate large bowl, mix together equal parts of:
- family time
- friend time
- Casey time

Slowly add content of medium bowl, and beat at top speed.

Pour into a Bundt pan coated with cleverness and

quick wit.

Bake 1/2 hour, and once cooled, add frosting, which consists of equal parts:

- silent, uncontrollable laughter
- adventure
- aunt love
- nephew hugs
- show tunes

Decorate all over with sprinkles of goofiness.

Serves 12, 0 calories, 0 carbs, no fat!!

Now write yours....

_____

_____

_____

_____

_____

_____

_____

_____

_____

_____

_____

_____

_____

_____

_____

_____

_____

_____

_____

_____

_____

Chapter 29:
MOJO Manifesto

"You get whatever accomplishment you are willing to declare."
~ Georgia O'Keeffe

This is a declaration of willingness to own your gifts, be bold, be seen, and take up space. Fill in the blanks and make a copy to refer to. Look at this MOJO Manifesto whenever you need a boost! Like Mufasa said in *The Lion King*, "Remember WHO YOU ARE!"

I, _____, do solemnly swear to work my MOJO with wild abandon. I will no longer hide my capacity for _____ and _____ because of my fear of _____. I am a fierce _____ who magically _____ with my own original style. When I _____, joy erupts in my soul. I vow to stop hiding my _____, because that would be an insult to my higher power that bestowed these gifts of _____ and _____ upon me. Therefore, I will begin offering the world my _____ today. When I feel MOJO-less, I will put on my theme song _____, do my happy dance, and connect with the MOJO that resides in my heart. Bust a move.

Francesca's MOJO Manifesto Example

I, Francesca, do solemnly swear to work my MOJO with wild abandon. I will no longer hide my capacity for becoming intuitive and powerful because of my fear of failing. I am a fierce Viking woman who magically shines with my own original style. When I dance, joy erupts in my soul. I vow to stop hiding my talents, because that would be an insult to my higher power that bestowed these gifts of energy and touch upon me. Therefore, I will begin offering the world my joy today. When I feel MOJO-less, I will put on my theme song "You Spin Me Round," do my happy dance, and connect with the MOJO that resides in my heart. Bust a move.

Chapter 30:
You Are a MOJO Beast

"There is a vitality, a life force, an energy, a quickening that is translated through you into action, and because there is only one of you in all of time, this expression is unique. And if you block it, it will never exist through any other medium and it will be lost. The world will not have it. It is not your business to determine how good it is nor how valuable nor how it compares with other expressions. It is your business to keep it yours clearly and directly, to keep the channel open. You do not even have to believe in yourself or your work. You have to keep yourself open and aware to the urges that motivate you. Keep the channel open...No artist is pleased. There is no satisfaction whatever at any time. There is only a queer divine dissatisfaction, a blessed unrest that keeps us marching and makes us more alive than the others."
~ Martha Graham

Congratulations! You have successfully completed your MOJO quest by doing the exercises in this book—right? Please tell me you've actually done the exercises. If you haven't, **DO THEM RIGHT NOW!** MOJO requires action! It would be like hoping to become physically fit by sitting on your couch while watching an exercise video.

If you've done the exercises, you have discovered your Magical, Original, Joyful Offering to the world! You've figured out what MOJO killers to be on the lookout for and the antidotes to save yourself should you ever ingest the poison again! You've mined for MOJO, picked your theme song, locked up your inner bully, changed your mindset, magnified your MOJO, and concocted your MOJO potion. GREAT JOB!!! You are now an official rock star! A badass. A bad mamajama. A master of MOJO. You are ready for your final task.

Here is your mission, should you choose to accept it: Get out there and stop hiding. Unveil the MOJO beast within you by casting off the shackles of doubt, shame, and conformity. Our world needs you to show up fully and fulfill your destiny. We all reap the rewards of your special MOJO potion. We need your art, your product, your wisdom, your zest, your skill, your expertise, your humor, your truth, and your love.

Be 100% you, MOJO beast. Your full and focused presence is requested—no, it's required. You are unique and have qualities that need to be expressed or you would not be here!

We need your courage and your unapologetic youness to thrive. Brandish your MOJO with all that your mama gave you and be an emissary of light and goodwill. Shine your light so bright that you are a beacon for all to see. You are a miracle, an expression of the divine, and the physical manifestation of all that is. If there are a few who do not appreciate your MOJO, they can suck it. Bless them and go on your merry way.

I am waving goodbye to you for now, MOJO beast. I am dressed as Diana Ross in my mother's polyester nightgown, holding my jump-rope microphone and singing to you…. "*If you need me, call me. No matter where you are, no matter how far.*"

As I float away in a pink bubble of disco delight, remember that I knew you had it in you all along. Go forth and be your magical, original, joyful self and offer it up to the world.

We're waiting.

Acknowledgments

This was such a monumental project for me—I'm a huge extrovert who loves people, not sitting alone behind my computer! I received so much encouragement to bring this book to life and for that I am eternally grateful. The concept for this book came to me on the ride home from an *O: The Oprah Magazine* conference in Los Angeles in 2012. In a burst of inspiration, I typed the outline into my phone while shouting out my ideas to my husband, my partner in crime for twenty-six years. So, first, thank you to "husbando" Alex for tirelessly urging me on, soothing my fears, and helping me believe in myself and my message—and especially for having a much bigger vision for me and this book than I could ever dream on my own.

Thank you to my book coach, editor, and friend Laura Wooten for being my ever-so-loving writing dominatrix, sounding board, and conspirator in bringing MOJO to the masses.

Thank you to my proofreader and co-editor extraordinaire Lynn Blaney Hess for saving my ass by polishing my work and helping me say what I really meant to say!

Thank you to my family for your support and love: my wonderful and funny sons Tyler and Cristian, my sister Dana, bro- in-law JD, nephews Soren and Rhys, and my mama-in-law Carole.

Thank you to my furry writing buddies—Teddy and Penny, my Yorkshire terriers—for making sure I was never really alone in the writing process!

Thank you to my dear friends Mary Welty-Dapkus, Laura Rosenberg, Chellie and Mike Kammermeyer, Carolyn and Mark Ulitsky, Jill Arburn, Shelley Mears, Kirsten Cameron, Marlice Miller, Karen Cooper, Lauren Pinnella, Cyndi MacKenzie, Gwen Kazemi, Laura Parisi, and Linda Dowell.

Thank you to Martha Beck and our MBI Coaching Tribe for your inspiration, wisdom, and experience. Thank you to all the people who let me pick their brain about the book writing and publishing process.

Finally, to my clients—thank you from the bottom of my heart for your transparency, vulnerability, willingness, tenacity, and trust. You motivate me to be more daring, more courageous, and to dream bigger. Your courage inspires me every day and I am blessed to be a part of your transformation. Thank you!